TAKE COURAGE

PSALMS OF SUPPORT AND ENCOURAGEMENT

EDITED BY
William J. Byron, S.J.

SHEED & WARD

Sheed & Ward™ is a service of The National Catholic Reporter Publishing Company.

LIBRARY OF CONGRESS CATALOGUING-IN-PUBLICATION DATA

Byron, S.J., William J.
ISBN: 1-55612-751-0

Published by: Sheed & Ward
115 E. Armour Blvd.
P.O. Box 419492
Kansas City, MO 64141

To order, call: (800) 333-7373

Cover design by Emil Antonucci.

Interior illustrations from Sheed & Ward's Clip Art publications: Meinrad Craighead's *Liturgical Art* (1988) and (p. 129) Lavrans Nielsen's *Sacred Art of Lavrans Nielsen* (1992).

Contents

ACKNOWLEDGMENTS

The thought of assembling this "psalter" occurred to me while I was working, with support from the Lilly Endowment, Inc., on a larger study of job loss among mid-career managers—men and women, 40 to 55 years of age, who found themselves "in transition" as a result of corporate downsizing. The complete study is available under the title, *Finding Work Without Losing Heart: Bouncing Back from Mid-Career Job Loss* (Holbrook, MA: Bob Adams, Inc., Publishers, 1995).

Among other things in the lives of those I interviewed, I looked at the relevance of religion. For some, "spirituality" was the operative word. Many mentioned the psalms as sources of encouragement and spiritual strength. I am grateful to the participants in my study for their cooperation, to the Lilly Endowment, Inc. for its support, and to the holder of the translation copyright for permission to use the selections from scripture that are published here.

Psalm texts used in this work are excerpted from *The Revised Psalms of the New American Bible*, Copyright 1991, The Confraternity of Christian Doctrine, Inc. All rights reserved.

"*Oremus pro invicem*," ("Let us pray for each other") is a traditional "sign-off" phrase that Jesuit letter-writers often employ in correspondence with one another. I use it now to convey prayerful best wishes to those who use this book, and to suggest that they remember in their prayers others whose burdens may be heavier than their own.

WJB
Georgetown University
Spring, 1994

TAKE COURAGE

PSALMS OF SUPPORT AND ENCOURAGEMENT

INTRODUCTION

During the latter part of 1992 and most of 1993, I studied the widespread problem of mid-career executive unemployment in corporate America. I spoke with managerial men and women who experienced first-hand the meaning of "downsizing" and "restructuring," new words for the old reality of layoff and unemployment. I interviewed many displaced white-collar workers and found that they hurt in the same vulnerable places where blue-collar workers feel the pain of job loss. Not just the wallet or bank account, but in stomach knots, and heavy hearts, and in soul-deep fears of never working again.

One of the realities I examined in their transition from one job to another was the relevance of religion in their lives. I inquired about a lot of things, including what they did or read to shore up their spirits. The psalms were often mentioned as sources of spiritual encouragement and support. To anyone who is a believer, and who has also experienced mid-career unemployment, this will come as no surprise.

Unemployment is a test of faith. The waiting, the uncertainty and anxiety over the unknown duration of enforced idleness, and the loss of control over your economic security— the whole experience of unemployment tests your faith in self and faith in God.

You have to believe in yourself, or you lose your sense of human dignity. Unemployment shakes your faith in self and sets off an erosion of self-esteem. You have to remind yourself, when you are out of work, that you are a human being, not a human doing; that your worth relates to who you are, not to what you have or what you do. Similarly, you have to reassert your faith in God; not just your belief that God exists, but that God exists with you here and now at your side, at this moment of distress, in your circumstances of joblessness.

The Psalter can serve as a prayer book for any believer; it can be particularly helpful to the unemployed. Persons who are out of work can easily get down on themselves and angry with God. The psalmist knew those human feelings; the psalms wrap words around the unexpressed thoughts that roil the emotions of persons in distress. Scripture is a "two-edged sword" (Heb. 4:12). The inspired words can be heard as God's voice speaking to you, saying, for example, "take courage; be stouthearted" (Ps. 27), and they can be used as your words spoken to God. The Spirit of God can pray within you in the words of the psalms. "When we read inspired texts, we go to school with the Holy Spirit," writes Luis Alonso Schokel, S.J., professor of Old Testament studies at the Pontifical Biblical Institute in Rome. This "schooling" can instruct you in both the ways of God and the wavering of the human spirit.

When you pick up the Bible, not to read but to pray, you are making an act of faith. Without faith, scripture is an unlighted torch, a vacant page, an empty envelope. With faith, the inspired word of God, preserved for you in the sacred scriptures, is a source of wisdom, consolation, and strength. Your faith is an affirmation of the divine reality that lies, quite literally, beyond you (even though you know, and know only by faith, that divine life and love are there within you). It is an immeasurable reality, the reality of God, and so is your dependence on God—all the time, not just when you're out of work. Faith is the climate within which you can forget the measurements and all the other tangibles, and simply entrust yourself to God. That is what you have to do when your faith is being tested by unemployment.

Speaking specifically of the psalms, the Carmelite scholar Roland Murphy acknowledges their universal appeal and practical utility for any believer: "For in these prayers is expressed the basic reactions of (the human person) before God—faith, joy, fear, trust, and praise—language no one can fail to understand."

The pages that follow put an edited version of selected psalms in the hands of persons who are in danger of losing heart. This booklet is for any believer under any stress, al-

4

though it owes its origins to the experience of persons undergoing the stress of unemployment. It will be helpful to anyone who is fearful or anxious for any reason at all. It is likely to work best if used on a one-psalm-a-day basis, letting the word of God function as a steady support for the day-by-day effort of finding a job, living with discouragement, or dealing with other stressful challenges.

At the beginning and end of each selection offered in these pages, there is a line that would traditionally be called an antiphon. This is a familiar liturgical term indicating a short verse sung at the opening and close of the sacred songs (psalms) in choral settings. The selections in this book will not be sung in liturgical settings, as the psalms were originally intended to be used. Nor, in most cases, will these selections be recited aloud, although the shorter ones will work well as "nondenominational" opening prayers at meetings of support groups.

In most instances, these adaptations from the Psalter will be prayed and pondered privately. So the lead-in verse, the "antiphon," is intended here to function as a keynote, or theme-line. Think of it as a faith-marker, a focal point, a motto, or guideline that can be internalized. It can be breathed in and breathed out, so to speak, prayerfully, and thus revive the spirits of the dejected but struggling believer.

The translation of the psalms used in the following pages is that of *The New American Bible*, where an introductory essay and footnotes can be found that will enhance the user's understanding of the context, as well as of the images and meaning conveyed by the words employed by those who wrote the psalms during the several-century period of their composition.

If you approach these words with faith, they, seedlike, will take root within you and grow. As you find this happening within you—by God's grace—you will notice your renewed capacity to "take courage" and "be stouthearted" in the face of unemployment, or any other trouble that comes your way.

William J. Byron, S.J.
Georgetown University
Spring, 1994

5

FROM PSALM 1

The LORD watches over the way of the just.

> Happy those who do not follow
> the counsel of the wicked,
> Nor go the way of sinners,
> nor sit in the company with scoffers.
> Rather, the law of the LORD is their
> joy. . . .
> They are like a tree
> planted near streams of water,
> that yields its fruit in season;
> Its leaves never wither;
> whatever they do prospers. . . .
> The LORD watches over the way of
> the just. . . .

The LORD watches over the way of the just.

FROM PSALM 2

Happy are all who take refuge in God.

> Why do the nations protest
> and the peoples grumble in vain?
>
> . . . .
>
> I will proclaim the decree of the
> LORD,
> who said to me, "You are my son;
> today I am your father.
> Only ask it of me,
> and I will make your inheritance
> the nations. . . ."
> Happy are all who take refuge in God.

Happy are all who take refuge in God.

FROM PSALM 3

But you, LORD, are a shield around me.

How many are my foes, LORD!
How many rise against me!

. . . .

But you, LORD, are a shield
around me;
my glory, you keep my head
high.
Whatever I cried out to the LORD,
I was answered from the holy
mountain.
Whenever I lay down and slept,
the LORD preserved me to rise
again.
I do not fear, then, thousands of
people
arrayed against me on every side.
Arise, LORD, save me, my God!
Safety comes from the LORD!

But you, LORD, are a shield around me.

FROM PSALM 4

Answer when I call, my saving God.

> Answer when I call, my saving God.
>   In my troubles, you cleared a way;
>   show me favor; hear my prayer. . . .
> Know that the LORD works wonders
>   for the faithful;
>   the LORD hears when I call out. . . .
> Offer fitting sacrifice
>   and trust in the LORD. . . .
> You have given my heart more
>   joy
>   than [others] have when grain and
>   wine abound. . . .
>   for you alone, LORD, make me secure.

Answer when I call, my saving God.

From Psalm 5

Hear my cry for help, my king, my God.

> Hear my words, O Lord;
>   listen to my sighing.
> Hear my cry for help,
>   my king, my God!
> To you I pray, O Lord;
>   at dawn you will hear my cry;
>   at dawn I will plead before you
>   and wait.
> You are not a god who delights in
>   evil;
>   no wicked person finds refuge
>   with you;
>   the arrogant cannot stand before
>   you. . . .
> But I can enter your house
>   because of your great love. . . .
> Guide me in your justice because of
>   my foes;
>   make straight your way before
>   me. . . .
> For you, Lord, bless the just;
>   you surround them with favor like
>   a shield.

Hear my cry for help, my king, my God.

FROM PSALM 6

Have pity on me, LORD, for I am weak.

>Do not reprove me in your anger,
>LORD,
>nor punish me in your wrath.
>Have pity on me, LORD, for I am
>weak;
>heal me, LORD, for my bones are
>trembling.
>In utter terror is my soul—
>and you, LORD, how long?

. . . .

>Turn, LORD, save my life;
>in your mercy rescue me.
>I am wearied with sighing;
>all night long tears drench my
>bed;
>my couch is soaked with weeping.
>My eyes are dimmed with sorrow,
>worn out because of all my foes.
>Away from me, all who do evil!
>The LORD has heard my weeping.
>The LORD has heard my prayer;
>the LORD takes up my plea.

Have pity on me, LORD, for I am weak.

FROM PSALM 7

A shield before me is God who saves the honest heart.

> Lord my God, in you I take refuge;
>> rescue me; save me from all who
>> pursue me,
>
> Lest they maul me like lions,
>> tear me to pieces with none to
>> save. . . .
>
> Grant me justice, Lord, for I am
> blameless,
>> free of any guilt.
>
> Bring the malice of the wicked to
> an end;
>> uphold the innocent,
>
> O God of justice,
>> who tries hearts and minds.
>
> A shield before me is God
>> who saves the honest heart. . . .
>
> I praise the justice of the Lord;
>> I celebrate the name of the Lord
>> Most High.

A shield before me is God who saves the honest heart.

FROM PSALM 8

O LORD, our LORD, how awesome is your name
through all the earth!

> O LORD, our LORD,
>> how awesome is your name
>> through all the earth!
>>> . . . .
>> When I see your heavens, the work
>>> of your fingers,
>> the moon and stars that you set
>>> in place—
>> What are humans that you are
>>> mindful of them,
>> mere mortals that you care for
>>> them?
>> Yet you have made them little less
>>> than a god,
>>> crowned them with glory and
>>>> honor.
>> You have given them rule over the
>>> works of your hands. . . .
>> O LORD, our LORD,
>>> how awesome is your name
>>> through all the earth!

O LORD, our LORD, how awesome is your name
through all the earth!

FROM PSALMS 9-10

To you [LORD] the helpless can entrust their cause.

> I will praise you, LORD, with all my
>   heart;
> I will declare all your wondrous
>   deeds.
> I will delight and rejoice in you;
>   I will sing hymns to your name,
>   Most High. . . .
> You upheld my right and my cause,
>   seated on your throne, judging
>   justly. . . .
> The LORD rules forever,
>   has set up a throne for judgment.
> It is God who governs the world with
>   justice,
>   who judges the people with fairness.
> The LORD is a stronghold for the
>   oppressed,
>   a stronghold in times of trouble.
> Those who honor your name trust
>   in you;
> you never forsake those
>   who seek you, LORD. . . .
> Have mercy on me, LORD;
>   see how my foes afflict me!

You alone can raise me from the
gates of death. . . .
Why, LORD, do you stand at a
distance
and pay no heed to these troubled
times?

. . . .

In their insolence the wicked boast:
"God doesn't care, doesn't even
exist."

. . . .

They lurk in ambush like lions in a
thicket,
hide there to trap the poor,
snare them and close the net.
The helpless are crushed, laid low;
they fall into the power of the
wicked,
Who say in their hearts, "God pays
no attention,
shows no concern, never bothers
to look."
Rise up, LORD God! Raise your arm!
Do not forget the poor!
Why should the wicked scorn God,
say in their hearts, "God doesn't
care?"

But you do see;
  you do observe this misery and
  sorrow;
  you take the matter in hand.
To you the helpless can entrust their
  cause. . . .
You listen, Lord, to the needs of the
  poor;
you encourage them and hear
  their prayers. . . .

To you [Lord] the helpless can entrust their cause.

FROM PSALM 11

In the LORD I take refuge.

> **In the LORD I take refuge;**
> **how can you say to me,**
> **"Flee like a bird to the**
> **mountains!"**
>
> . . . .
>
> **The LORD is just and loves just**
> **deeds;**
> **the upright shall see his face.**

In the LORD I take refuge.

FROM PSALM 12

Help, LORD, for no one loyal remains.

> Help, LORD, for no one loyal
> remains;
> the faithful have vanished from
> the human race. . . .
> "I will now arise," says the LORD;
> "I will grant safety to whoever
> longs for it."
> The promises of the LORD are sure,
> [like] silver refined in a crucible,
> silver purified seven times.
> LORD, protect us always. . . .

Help, LORD, for no one loyal remains.

FROM PSALM 13

Look upon me, answer me, LORD, my God!

> How long, LORD? Will you utterly
> forget me?
> How long will you hide your face
> from me?
> How long must I carry sorrow in my
> soul,
>> grief in my heart day after day?

> . . . .

> Look upon me, answer me, LORD,
> my God!

> . . . .

> I trust in your faithfulness.
> Grant my heart joy in your help,
> That I may sing of the LORD,
>> "How good our God has been to
>> me!"

Look upon me, answer me, LORD, my God.

FROM PSALM 14

The LORD restores his people.

> Fools say in their hearts,
> "There is no God."
>
> . . . .
>
> The LORD looks down from heaven
> upon the human race,
> To see if even one is wise,
> if even one seeks God. . . .
> The poor have the LORD as
> their refuge. . . .
> the LORD restores his people!

The LORD restores his people.

From Psalm 16

Keep me safe, O God; in you I take refuge.

> Keep me safe, O God;
> in you I take refuge.
> I say to the LORD.
> you are my LORD,
> you are my only good. . . .
> LORD, my allotted portion and my cup,
> you have made my destiny secure. . . .
> I bless the LORD who counsels me;
> even at night my heart exhorts me.
> I keep the LORD always before me;
> with the LORD at my right,
> I shall never be shaken.
> Therefore, my heart is glad, my soul
> rejoices;
> my body also dwells secure,
> For you will not abandon me to
> Sheol [the pit],
> nor let your faithful servant see
> the pit.
> You will show me the path to life,
> abounding joy in your presence,
> the delights at your right hand forever.

Keep me safe, O God; in you I take refuge.

FROM PSALM 17

I call upon you; answer me, O God.

> Hear, LORD, my plea for justice;
> pay heed to my cry;
> Listen to my prayer
> spoken without guile.
> From you let my vindication come;
> your eyes see what is right.
> You have tested my heart,
> searched it in the night.
> You have tried me by fire.
> but find no malice in me.
> My mouth has not transgressed
> as humans often do.
> As your lips have instructed me,
> I have kept the way of the law.
> My steps have kept to your paths;
> my feet have not faltered.
> I call upon you; answer me, O God.
> Turn your ear to me; hear my
> prayer.
> Show your wonderful love,
> you who deliver with your right arm
> those who seek refuge from their foes.
> Keep me as the apple of your eye;
> hide me in the shadow of your wings

from the violence of the wicked. . . .
I am just—let me see your face;
when I awake, let me be filled
with your presence.

I call upon you; answer me, O God.

FROM PSALM 18

In my distress I called out, LORD!
I cried out to my God.

> I love you, LORD, my strength,
> LORD, my rock, my fortress, my
> deliverer,
> My God, my rock of refuge,
> my shield, my saving horn, my
> stronghold. . . .
> The breakers of death surged round
> about me;
> the menacing floods terrified me.
> The cords of Sheol tightened;
> the snares of death lay in wait
> for me.
> In my distress I called out, LORD!
> I cried out to my God.
> From his temple he heard my voice. . . .
> He parted the heavens and came down,
> a dark cloud under his feet.
> Mounted on a cherub he flew,
> borne along on the wings of the
> wind.
> He made darkness the cover about him;
> his canopy, heavy thunderheads.
> Before him scudded his clouds,

hail and lightning, too.
The LORD thundered from heaven;
  the Most High made his voice resound. . . .
Then the bed of the sea appeared;
  the world's foundations lay bare,
At the roar of the LORD,
  at the storming breath of his nostrils.
He reached down from on high and
  seized me;
    drew me out of the deep waters.
He rescued me from my mighty enemy,
  from foes too powerful for me. . . .
He set me free in the open;
  he rescued me because he loves me. . . .
You, LORD, give light to my lamp;
  my God brightens the darkness
  about me.
With you I can rush an armed band,
  with my God to help I can leap a wall.
God's way is unerring,
  the LORD's promise is tried and true;
  he is a shield for all who trust in him.
Truly, who is God except the LORD?
  Who but our God is the rock?
This God who girded me with might,
  kept my way unerring,
Who made my feet swift as a deer's,

set me safe on the heights. . . .
You have given me your protecting
 shield;
  your right hand has upheld me;
  you stooped to make me great.
You gave me room to stride;
  my feet never stumbled. . . .
Truly you have exalted me above
 my adversaries,
  from the violent you have rescued me.
Thus I will proclaim you, LORD,
  among the nations;
  I will sing the praises of your name.

In my distress I called out, LORD!
I cried out to my God.

FROM PSALM 20

The LORD grant your every prayer.

> The LORD answer you in time of
> distress;
> the name of the God of Jacob
> defend you!
> May God send you help from the
> temple,
> from Zion be your support.
> May God . . . grant what is in your
> heart,
> fulfill your every plan.
> May we shout for joy at your victory,
> raise the banners in the name of
> our God.
> The LORD grant your every prayer!
> Now I know victory is given
> to the anointed of the LORD.
> God will answer him from the holy
> heavens
> with a strong arm that brings victory.
> Some rely on chariots, others on horses,
> but we on the name of the LORD our God.
> They collapse and fall,
> but we stand strong and firm. . . .

The LORD grant your every prayer.

FROM PSALM 22

But you, LORD, do not stay far off;
my strength, come quickly to help me.

> My God, my God, why have you
> abandoned me?
> Why so far from my call for help,
> from my cries of anguish?
> My God, I call by day, but you
> do not answer;
> by night, but I have no relief.
> Yet you are enthroned as the Holy One;
> you are the glory of Israel.
> In you our ancestors trusted;
> they trusted and you rescued them.
> To you they cried out and they escaped;
> in you they trusted and were
> not disappointed.
> But I am a worm, hardly human,
> scorned by everyone, despised by
> the people.
> All who see me mock me;
> they curl their lips and jeer;
> they shake their heads at me:
> "You relied on the LORD—let him
> deliver you;
> if he loves you, let him rescue you."

Yet you drew me forth from the womb,
made me safe at my mother's breast.
Upon you I was thrust from the womb;
since birth you are my God.
Do not stay far from me,
for trouble is near,
and there is no one to help. . . .
Like water my life drains away;
all my bones grow soft.
My heart has become like wax,
it melts away within me. . . .
But you, LORD, do not stay far off;
my strength, come quickly to help me. . . .
Save me from the lion's mouth,
my poor life from the horns of wild bulls.
Then I will proclaim your name to
the assembly;
in the community I will praise you. . . .
For God has not spurned or disdained
the misery of this poor wretch,
but heard me when I cried out.

But you, LORD, do not stay far off;
my strength, come quickly to help me.

FROM PSALM 23

Even when I walk through a dark valley,
I fear no harm for you are at my side.

> The LORD is my shepherd;
> > there is nothing I lack.
> In green pastures you let me graze;
> > to safe waters you lead me;
> > you restore my strength.
> You guide me along the right path
> > for the sake of your name.
> Even when I walk through a dark valley,
> > I fear no harm for you are at my side;
> > your rod and staff give me courage.
> You set a table before me
> > as my enemies watch;
> You anoint my head with oil;
> > my cup overflows.
> Only goodness and love will pursue me
> > all the days of my life;
> I will dwell in the house of the LORD
> > for years to come.

Even when I walk through a dark valley,
I fear no harm for you are at my side.

FROM PSALM 24

The earth is the LORD'S
and all it holds.

> The earth is the LORD's and all it
> holds,
> the world and those who live
> there.
> For God founded it on the seas,
> established it over the rivers.
> Who may go up the mountain
> of the LORD?
> [Those] who are not devoted
> to idols,
> who have not sworn falsely.
> They will receive blessings
> from the LORD.

The earth is the LORD'S
and all it holds.

FROM PSALM 25

In you I trust; do not let me be disgraced.

> I wait for you, O LORD;
>   I lift up my soul to my God.
> In you I trust; do not let me be
>   disgraced;
>   do not let my enemies gloat over me.
> No one is disgraced who waits for you,
>   but only those who lightly
>   break faith.
> Make known to me your ways, LORD;
>   teach me your paths.
> Guide me in your truth and
>   teach me,
>   for you are God, my savior.
> For you I wait all the long day,
>   because of your goodness, LORD.
> Remember your compassion and
>   love, O LORD;
>   for they are ages old.
> Remember no more the sins of
>   my youth;
>   remember me only in light of
>   your love.
> Good and upright is the LORD.
>   who shows sinners the way,

Guides the humble rightly,
  and teaches the humble the way. . . .
For the sake of your name, LORD,
  pardon my guilt, though it is great.
Who are those who fear the LORD?
  God shows them the way to choose.
They live well and prosper,
  and their descendants inherit the land.
The counsel of the LORD belongs to
  the faithful;
  the covenant instructs them.
My eyes are ever upon the LORD,
  who frees my feet from the snare.
Look upon me, have pity on me,
  for I am alone and afflicted.
Relieve the troubles of my heart;
  bring me out of my distress.
Put an end to my affliction and
  suffering;
  take away all my sins. . . .
Preserve my life and rescue me;
  do not let me be disgraced,
  for I trust in you.
Let honesty and virtue preserve me;
  I wait for you, O LORD. . . .

In you I trust; do not let me be disgraced.

FROM PSALM 26

I walk guided by your faithfulness.

> Grant me justice, LORD!
> I have walked without blame.
> In the LORD I have trusted;
> I have not faltered.
> Test me, LORD, and try me;
> search my heart and mind.
> Your love is before my eyes;
> I walk guided by your
> faithfulness. . . .

I walk guided by your faithfulness.

FROM PSALM 27

Take courage; be stouthearted,
wait for the LORD.

The LORD is my light and my salvation;
whom do I fear?
The LORD is my life's refuge;
of whom am I afraid?

. . . .

Though an army encamp against me,
my heart does not fear;
Though war be waged against me,
even then do I trust.
One thing I ask of the LORD;
this I seek:
To dwell in the LORD's house
all the days of my life,
To gaze on the LORD's beauty,
to visit his temple.
For God will hide me in his shelter
in time of trouble.
Will conceal me in the cover of his
tent;
and set me high upon a rock.
Even now my head is held high. . . .
Hear my voice, LORD, when I call;
have mercy on me and answer me.

"Come," says my heart, "seek God's
 face";
   your face, LORD, do I seek!
Do not hide your face from me;
   do not repel your servant in anger.
You are my help; do not cast me off;
   do not forsake me, God, my savior!
Even if my father and mother forsake me,
   the LORD will take me in.
LORD, show me your way;
   lead me on a level path. . . .
Do not abandon me to the will
   of my foes. . . .
But I believe I shall enjoy the LORD's
 goodness
   in the land of the living.
Wait for the LORD, take courage;
   be stouthearted, wait for the LORD.

Take courage; be stouthearted,
wait for the LORD.

FROM PSALM 28

LORD, you are the strength of your people.

> To you, LORD, I call;
>> my Rock, do not be deaf to me.
>
> If you fail to answer me,
>> I will join those who go down
>> to the pit.
>
> Hear the sound of my pleading when
>> I cry to you,
>> lifting my hands toward your holy
>> place. . . .
>
> Blessed be the LORD,
>> who has heard the sound of my
>> pleading.
>
> The LORD is my strength and my shield,
>> in whom my heart trusted and found help.
>
> So my heart rejoices;
>> with my song I praise my God.
>
> LORD, you are the strength of your people,
>> the saving refuge of your anointed king.
>
> Save your people, bless your inheritance;
>> feed and sustain them forever!

LORD, you are the strength of your people.

From Psalm 30

LORD, be my helper.

> I praise you, LORD, for you raised me up
> and did not let my enemies rejoice
> over me.
> O LORD, my God,
> I cried out to you and you healed me.
> LORD, you brought me up from Sheol;
> you kept me from going down
> to the pit. . . .
> Complacent, I once said,
> "I shall never be shaken."
> LORD, when you showed me favor
> I stood like the mighty mountains.
> But when you hid your face
> I was struck with terror.
> To you, LORD, I cried out;
> with the LORD I pleaded for mercy:
> "What gain is there from my lifeblood,
> from my going down to the grave?
> Does dust give you thanks
> or declare your faithfulness?
> Hear, O LORD, have mercy on me;
> LORD, be my helper."
> You changed my mourning into dancing;
> you took off my sackcloth

and clothed me with gladness.
With my whole being I sing
   endless praise to you.
O LORD, my God,
   forever will I give you thanks.

LORD, be my helper.

FROM PSALM 31

Be gracious to me, LORD, for I am in distress.

In you, LORD, I take refuge;
let me never be put to shame.
In your justice deliver me;
incline your ear to me;
make haste to rescue me!
Be my rock of refuge.
a stronghold to save me.
You are my rock and my fortress;
for your name's sake lead me and
guide me.
Free me from the net they have set
for me,
for you are my refuge.
Into your hands I commend my spirit;
you will redeem me, LORD, faithful God. . . .
I will rejoice and be glad in your love,
once you have seen my misery,
observed my distress.
You will not abandon me into enemy hands,
but will set my feet in a free and
open space.
Be gracious to me, LORD, for I am
in distress;
with grief my eyes are wasted,

my soul and body spent.
My life is worn out by sorrow,
my years by sighing.
My strength fails in affliction;
my bones are consumed. . . .
I am forgotten, out of mind
like the dead;
I am like a shattered dish.
I hear the whispers of the crowd;
terrors are all around me. . . .
But I trust in you, LORD;
I say, "You are my God."
My times are in your hands;
rescue me from my enemies,
from the hands of my pursuers.
Let your face shine on your servant,
save me in your kindness.
Do not let me be put to shame,
for I have called to you, LORD. . . .
How great is your goodness, LORD,
stored up for those who fear you.
You display it for those who trust you,
in the sight of all the people.
You hide them in the shelter of your
presence,
safe from scheming enemies.
You keep them in your abode,

safe from plotting tongues.

Blessed be the LORD,

who has shown me wondrous love,

and been for me a city most

secure. . . .

Be strong and take heart,

all you who hope in the LORD.

Be gracious to me, LORD, for I am in distress.

FROM PSALM 32

You are my shelter; from distress you keep me.

> Happy the sinner whose fault is
> removed,
> whose sin is forgiven.
> Happy those to whom the LORD
> imputes no guilt,
> in whose spirit is no deceit.
> As long as I kept silent, my bones
> wasted away;
> I groaned all the day.
> For day and night your hand was
> heavy upon me;
> my strength withered as in dry
> summer heat.
> Then I declared my sin to you;
> my guilt I did not hide.
> I said, "I confess my faults to
> the LORD,"
> and you took away the guilt
> of my sin.
> Thus should all the faithful pray
> in time of distress.
> Though flood waters threaten,
> they will never reach them.
> You are my shelter; from distress

you keep me;

with safety you ring me round.

I will instruct you and show you the
way you should walk,

give you counsel and

watch over you. . . .

Be glad in the LORD and rejoice,
you just;

exult, all you upright of heart.

You are my shelter; from distress you keep me.

From Psalm 33

Our soul waits for the LORD,
who is our help and shield.

. . . .

    Sing to God a new song;
      skillfully play with joyful chant.
    For the LORD's word is true;
      all his works are trustworthy.
    The LORD loves justice and right
      and fills the earth with goodness.
    By the LORD's word the heavens
      were made;
      by the breath of his mouth
      all their host.
    The waters of the sea were gathered
      as in a bowl;
      in cellars the deep was confined.
    Let all the earth fear the LORD;
      let all who dwell in the world
      show reverence.
    For he spoke, and it came to be,
      commanded, and it stood in place. . . .
    The plan of the LORD stands forever,
      wise designs through all generations.
    Happy the nation whose God is the LORD,
      the people chosen as his very own.

From heaven the LORD looks down
and observes the whole human race,
surveying from the royal throne
all who dwell on earth.
The one who fashioned the hearts
of them all
knows all their works. . . .
The LORD's eyes are upon the reverent,
upon those who hope for his
gracious help,
Delivering them from death,
keeping them alive in times of famine.
Our soul waits for the LORD,
who is our help and shield.
For in God our hearts rejoice;
in your holy name we trust.
May your kindness, LORD, be upon us;
we have put our hope in you.

Our soul waits for the LORD,
who is our help and shield.

From Psalm 34

I sought the LORD, who answered me.

> I will bless the LORD at all times;
>> praise shall be always in my mouth.
>
> My soul will glory in the LORD
>> that the poor may hear and be glad.
>
> Magnify the LORD with me;
>> let us exult his name together.
>
> I sought the LORD, who answered me,
>> delivered me from all my fears.
>
> Look to God that you may be radiant
>> with joy
>> and your faces may not blush for shame.
>
> In my misfortune I called,
>> the LORD heard and saved me from
>> all my distress.
>
> The angel of the LORD who encamps
>> with them,
>> delivers all who fear God.
>
> Learn to savor how good the LORD is;
>> happy are those who take refuge in him.
>
> Fear the LORD, you holy ones;
>> nothing is lacking to those who
>> fear him.
>
> The powerful grow poor and hungry,
>> but those who seek the LORD lack no

good thing. . . .
Keep your tongue from evil,
   your lips from speaking lies.
Turn from evil and do good;
   seek peace and pursue it.
The LORD has eyes for the just
   and ears for their cry. . . .
When the just cry out,
   the LORD hears
   and rescues them from all distress.
The LORD is close to the brokenhearted,
   saves those whose spirit is crushed.
Many are the troubles of the just,
   but the LORD delivers from them all.
God watches over all their bones;
   not a one shall be broken. . . .

I sought the LORD, who answered me.

FROM PSALM 35

LORD, do not withdraw from me.

    . . . .[LORD,] say to my heart,
    "I am your salvation."
    Let those who seek my life
      be put to shame and disgrace.
    Let those who plot evil against me
      be turned back and confounded. . . .
    My very bones shall say,
    "O LORD, who is like you,
    Who rescue the afflicted from the
      powerful,
      the afflicted and needy from
      the despoiler?"

        . . . .

LORD, how long will you look on?
    Save me from the roaring beasts,
    my precious life from lions!
Then I will thank you in the great
    assembly;
    I will praise you before the mighty
    throng. . . .
LORD, do not withdraw from me.
Awake, be vigilant in my defense,
    in my cause, my God and my LORD.
Defend me because you are just, LORD;

my God, do not let them gloat over me. . . .
Put to shame and confound
  all who relish my misfortune. . . .
But let those who favor my just cause
  shout for joy and be glad.
May they ever say, "Exalted be the LORD
  who delights in the peace of his
  loyal servant."
Then my tongue shall recount your justice,
  declare your praise, all the day long.

LORD, do not withdraw from me.

FROM PSALM 36

We take refuge in the shadow of your wings.

> .... LORD, your love reaches to heaven;
> your fidelity to the clouds.
> Your justice is like the highest
> mountains;
> your judgments, like the mighty deep;
> all living creatures you sustain, LORD.
> How precious is your love, O God!
> We take refuge in the shadow of
> your wings.
> We feast on the rich food of your house;
> from your delightful stream, you give
> us drink.
> For with you is the fountain of life,
> and in your light we see light.
> Continue your kindness toward your friends,
> your just defense of the honest heart.
> Do not let the foot of the proud overtake me,
> nor the hand of the wicked disturb me. ...

We take refuge in the shadow of your wings.

From Psalm 37

Commit your way to the LORD;
trust that God will act.

> . . . .Trust in the LORD and do good
> that you may dwell in the land
> and live secure.
> Find your delight in the LORD
> who will give you your heart's desire.
> Commit your way to the LORD;
> trust that God will act
> And make your integrity shine like the dawn,
> your vindication like noonday.
> Be still before the LORD,
> wait for God. . . .
> Give up your anger, abandon your wrath;
> do not be provoked; it brings only harm.
> Those who do evil will be cut off,
> but those who wait for the LORD
> will possess the land.
> Wait a little, and the wicked will be
> no more.
> Look for them and they will not
> be there.
> But the poor will possess the land,
> will delight in great prosperity. . . .
> Better the poverty of the just

than the great wealth of the wicked.
The arms of the wicked will be broken;
  the LORD will sustain the just.
The LORD watches over the days of
  the blameless. . . .
Those whose steps are guided by the LORD,
  whose way God approves,
May stumble, but they will never fall,
  for the LORD holds their hand.
Neither in my youth, nor now in old age
  have I ever seen the just abandoned
  or their children begging bread.
The just always lend generously,
  and their children become a blessing.
Turn from evil and do good,
  that you may inhabit the land forever.
For the LORD loves justice
  and does not abandon the faithful. . . .
The mouths of the just utter wisdom;
  their tongues speak what is right.
God's teaching is in their hearts;
  their steps do not falter.
Wait eagerly for the LORD,
  and keep to the way;
God will raise you to possess the land. . . .
Observe the honest, mark the upright;
  those at peace with God have a future. . . .

The salvation of the just is from the LORD,
   their refuge in time of distress.
The LORD helps and rescues them from the
   wicked,
      because in God they take refuge.

Commit your way to the LORD;
trust that God will act.

FROM PSALM 38

LORD, I wait for you;
O LORD, my God, answer me.

> LORD, punish me no more in your anger;
>> in your wrath do not chastise me!
>
> Your arrows have sunk deep in me;
>> your hand has come down upon me.
>
> My flesh is afflicted because of your anger;
>> my frame aches because of my sin. . . .
>
> My LORD, my deepest yearning is before you;
>> my groaning is not hidden from you.
>
> My heart shudders, my strength forsakes me;
>> the very light of my eyes has failed.
>
> Friends and companions shun my pain;
>> my neighbors stand far off. . . .
>
> LORD, I wait for you;
>> O LORD, my God, answer me. . . .
>
> I am very near to falling;
>> my pain is with me always. . . .
>
> Forsake me not, O LORD;
>> my God, be not far from me!
>
> Come quickly to help me,
>> my LORD and my salvation.

LORD, I wait for you;
O LORD, my God, answer me.

FROM PSALM 39

And now, LORD, what future do I have?
You are my only hope.

> . . . . LORD, let me know my end,
> the number of my days,
>> that I may learn how frail I am.
>
> You have given my days a very short span;
>> my life is as nothing before you.
>> All mortals are but a breath.
>
> Mere phantoms, we go our way;
>> mere vapor, our restless pursuits;
>> we heap up stones without knowing
>> for whom.
>
> And now, LORD, what future do I have?
>> You are my only hope.
>
> From all my sins deliver me;
>> let me not be the taunt of fools. . . .
>
> Listen to my prayer, LORD, hear my cry;
>> do not be deaf to my weeping!
>
> I sojourn with you like a passing stranger,
>> a guest, like all my ancestors.
>
> Turn your gaze from me, that I may find peace
>> before I depart to be no more.

And now, LORD, what future do I have?
You are my only hope.

FROM PSALM 40

LORD, graciously rescue me!
Come quickly to help me, LORD!
 Happy those who trust in the LORD,
  who turn not to idolatry
  or to those who stray after falsehood.
 How numerous, O LORD, my God,
  you have made your wondrous deeds!
 And in your plans for us
  there is none to equal you.
 Should I wish to declare or tell them,
  too many are they to recount.
 Sacrifice and offering you do not want;
  but ears open to obedience you gave me.
 Holocausts and sin-offerings you do
  not require;
  so I said, "Here I am; your commands for me
  are written in the scroll.
 To do your will is my delight;
  my God, your law is in my heart!"
     . . . .
 LORD, do not withhold your compassion
  from me;
 may your enduring kindness
  ever preserve me.
 For all about me are evils beyond count;

my sins so overcome me I cannot see.
They are more than the hairs of my head;
 my courage fails me.
Lord, graciously rescue me!
 Come quickly to help me, Lord!

. . . .

May those who long for your help always say,
 "The Lord be glorified."
Though I am afflicted and poor,
 the Lord keeps me in mind.
You are my help and deliverer;
 my God, do not delay!

Lord, graciously rescue me!
Come quickly to help me, Lord!

FROM PSALMS 42-43

You, God, are my strength.

Why are you downcast, my soul;
   why do you groan within me?
Wait for God, whom I shall praise again,
   my savior and my God.
My soul is downcast within me;
   therefore I will remember you
From the land of Jordan and Hermon,
   from the land of Mount Mizar.
Here deep calls to deep in the roar
   of your torrents.
All your waves and breakers
   sweep over me.
At dawn may the LORD bestow faithful love
   that I may sing praise through the night,
   praise to the God of my life.
I say to God, "My rock,
   why do you forget me?
Why must I go about mourning
   with the enemy oppressing me?"
It shatters my bones, when my adversaries
   reproach me.
They say to me daily: "Where is your God?"
Why are you downcast, my soul,
   why do you groan within me?

Wait for God, whom I shall praise again,
   my savior and my God. . . .
You, God, are my strength.
   Why then do you spurn me?
Why must I go about mourning
   with the enemy oppressing me?
Send your light and fidelity
   that they may be my guide
And bring me to your holy mountain,
   to the place of your dwelling. . . .
Why are you downcast, my soul?
   Why do you groan within me?
Wait for God, whom I shall praise
   again,
   my savior and my God.

You, God, are my strength.

FROM PSALM 44

Awake! Why do you sleep, O LORD?

> O God, we have heard with our own ears;
>   our ancestors have told us
> The deeds you did in their days,
>   with your own hand in days of old:
> You rooted out nations to plant them,
>   crushed peoples to make room for them.
> Not with their own swords did they
>   conquer the land,
>   nor did their own arms bring victory;
> It was your right hand, your own arm,
>   the light of your face, for you
>   favored them. . . .
> Not in my bow do I trust,
>   nor does my sword bring me victory.
> You have brought us victory over
>   our enemies,
>   shamed those who hate us.
> In God we have boasted all the day long;
>   your name we will praise forever. . . .
> Our hearts have not turned back,
>   nor have our steps strayed from
>   your path.
> Yet you have left us crushed,
>   desolate in a place of jackals;

you have covered us with darkness.
If we had forgotten the name of our God,
  stretched out our hands to another god,
Would not God have discovered this,
  God who knows the secrets of the heart?

. . . .

Awake! Why do you sleep, O LORD?
  Rise up! Do not reject us forever!
Why do you hide your face;
  why forget our pain and misery?
We are bowed down to the ground;
  our bodies are pressed to the earth.
Rise up, help us!
  Redeem us as your love demands.

Awake! Why do you sleep, O LORD?

From Psalm 46

God is our refuge and our strength.

> God is our refuge and our strength,
> an ever present help in distress.
> Thus we do not fear, though earth
> be shaken
> and mountains quake to the
> depths of the sea;
> Though its waters rage and foam
> and mountains totter at its surging.
> The LORD of hosts is with us;
> our stronghold is the God of Jacob.
> Streams of the river gladden
> the city of God,
> the holy dwelling of the Most High.
> God is in its midst; it shall not
> be shaken;
> God will help it at break of day.
> Though nations rage and kingdoms totter,
> God's voice thunders and the
> earth trembles.
> The LORD of hosts is with us;
> our stronghold is the God of Jacob.
> Come and see the works of the LORD,
> who has done fearsome deeds on earth;
> Who stops wars to the ends of the earth,

breaks the bow, splinters the spear,
and burns the shields with fire;
Who says:
"Be still and confess that I am God!
I am exalted among the nations,
exalted on the earth."
The LORD of hosts is with us;
our stronghold is the God of Jacob.

God is our refuge and our strength.

From Psalm 48

O God, within your temple
we ponder your steadfast love.

> Great is the LORD and highly praised
>   in the city of our God. . . .
> God is its citadel,
>   renowned as a stronghold. . . .
> What we had heard we now see
>   in the city of the LORD of hosts,
> In the city of our God,
>   founded to last forever.
> O God, within your temple
>   we ponder your steadfast love. . . .
> The cities of Judah rejoice
>   because of your saving deeds!
>
>   . . . .
>
> Yes, so mighty is God,
>   our God who leads us always!

O God, within your temple
we ponder your steadfast love.

FROM PSALM 51

Renew in me a steadfast spirit.

> Have mercy on me, God, in your goodness,
>   in your abundant compassion blot
>   out my offense.
> Wash away all my guilt;
>   from my sin cleanse me.
> For I know my offense;
>   my sin is always before me.
> Against you alone have I sinned;
>   I have done such evil in your sight
> That you are just in your sentence,
>   blameless when you condemn.
> True, I was born guilty,
>   a sinner, even as my mother
>   conceived me.
> Still, you insist on sincerity of heart;
>   in my inmost being teach me wisdom.
> Cleanse me with hyssop, that I may be pure;
>   wash me, make me whiter than snow.
> Let me hear sounds of joy and gladness;
>   let the bones you have crushed rejoice.
> Turn away your face from my sins;
>   blot out all my guilt.
> A clean heart create for me, God;
>   renew in me a steadfast spirit.

Do not drive me from your presence,
nor take from me your holy spirit.
Restore my joy in your salvation;
sustain in me a willing spirit. . . .
Rescue me from death, God, my saving God,
that my tongue may praise your
healing power.
LORD, open my lips;
my mouth will proclaim your praise.
For you do not desire sacrifice;
a burnt offering you would not accept.
My sacrifice, God, is a broken spirit;
God, do not spurn a broken,
humbled heart. . . .

Renew in me a steadfast spirit.

From Psalm 54

God is present as my helper;
the LORD sustains my life.

> O God, by your name save me.
> By your strength
> defend my cause.
> O God, hear my prayer.
> Listen to the words
> of my mouth.
> The arrogant have risen
> against me;
> the ruthless seek my life. . . .
> God is present as my helper;
> the LORD sustains my life. . . .

God is present as my helper;
the LORD sustains my life.

From Psalm 55

Cast your care upon the LORD,
who will give you support.

> Listen, God, to my prayer;
>   do not hide from my pleading;
>   hear me and give answer.
> I rock with grief; I groan. . . .
> My heart pounds within me;
>   death's terrors fall upon me.
> Fear and trembling overwhelm me;
>   shuddering sweeps over me.
> I say, "If only I had wings like
> a dove,
>   that I might fly away
>   and find rest.
> Far away I would flee;
>   I would stay in the desert.
> I would soon find a shelter
>   from the raging wind and storm."
>
>   . . . .
>
> But I will call upon God,
>   and the LORD will save me.
> At dusk, dawn, and noon
>   I will grieve and complain,
>   and my prayer will be heard.
> God will give me freedom and peace

from those who war against me,
though there are many who
oppose me.
God, who sits enthroned forever,
will hear me and humble them. . . .
Cast your care upon the LORD,
who will give you support.
God will never allow
the righteous to stumble. . . .

Cast your care upon the LORD,
who will give you support.

FROM PSALM 56

This I know: God is on my side.

> Have mercy on me, God, for I am treated
> harshly; attackers press me all the day.
> My foes treat me harshly all the day;
>   yes, many are my attackers.
> O Most High, when I am afraid,
>   in you I place my trust.
> God, I praise your promise;
>   in you I trust, I do not fear.
>   What can mere flesh do to me?
> My wanderings you have noted;
>   are my tears not stored in your vial,
>   recorded in your book?
> My foes turn back when I call on you.
>   This I know; God is on my side.
> God, I praise your promise;
>   in you I trust, I do not fear.
>   What can mere mortals do to me?
> I have made vows to you, God;
>   with offerings I will fulfill them,
> Once you have snatched me from death,
>   kept my feet from stumbling,
> That I may walk before God
>   in the light of the living.

This I know: God is on my side.

FROM PSALM 57

May God send help from heaven to save me.

> Have mercy on me, God,
>> have mercy on me.
>> In you I seek shelter.
> In the shadow of your wings
>> I seek shelter
>> till harm pass by.
> I call to God Most High,
>> to God who provides for me.
> May God send help from heaven
>> to save me,
>> shame those who trample upon me.
>> May God send fidelity and love. . . .
> Show yourself over the heavens, God;
>> may your glory appear
>> above all the earth. . . .
> My heart is steadfast, God,
>> my heart is steadfast.
>> I will sing and chant praise.
> Awake, my soul;
>> awake, lyre and harp!
>> I will wake the dawn.
> I will praise you among the peoples,
>> LORD;
>> I will chant your praise

among the nations.
For your love towers to the heavens;
your faithfulness to the skies.
Show yourself over the heavens, God;
may your glory appear
above all the earth.

May God send help from heaven to save me.

FROM PSALM 59

For you are my fortress,
my refuge in time of trouble.

> Rescue me from my enemies, my God;
>   lift me out of reach of my foes.
> Deliver me from evildoers;
>   from the bloodthirsty save me.
> They have set an ambush for my life;
>   the powerful conspire against me.
> For no offense or misdeed of mine,
>   LORD,
>   for no fault they hurry to take up
>   arms.
> Come near and see my plight. . . .
> My strength, for you I watch;
>   you, God, are my fortress,
>   my loving God. . . .
> But I shall sing of your strength,
>   extol your love at dawn,
> For you are my fortress,
>   my refuge in time of trouble.
> My strength, your praises I will sing;
>   you, God, are my fortress,
>   my loving God.

For you are my fortress,
my refuge in time of trouble.

FROM PSALM 60

We will triumph with the help of God.

> O God, you rejected us, broke
> our defenses;
> you were angry but now revive us. . . .
> You made your people go through
> hardship,
> made us stagger from
> the wine you gave us. . . .
> Help with your right hand
> and answer us
> that you loved ones may escape. . . .
> Who will bring me to the fortified city?
> Who will lead me into Edom?
> Was it not you who rejected us, God?
> Do you no longer march with our armies?
> Give us aid against the foe;
> worthless is human help.
> We will triumph with the help of God. . . .

We will triumph with the help of God.

FROM PSALM 61

Hear my cry, O LORD,
listen to my prayer.

> Hear my cry, O LORD,
>   listen to my prayer!
> From the brink of Sheol I call,
>   my heart grows faint.
> Raise me up, set me on a rock,
>   for you are my refuge,
>   a tower of strength against
>   the foe.
> Then I will ever dwell
>   in your tent,
>   take refuge in the shelter
>   of your wings. . . .
> Then I will sing your name forever,
>   fulfill my vows day after day.

Hear my cry, O LORD,
listen to my prayer.

From Psalm 62

God alone is my rock and my salvation.

> My soul rests in God alone,
>   from whom comes my salvation.
> God alone is my rock and salvation,
>   my secure height; I shall never fall. . . .
> My soul, be at rest in God alone,
>   from whom comes my hope.
> God alone is my rock and my salvation,
>   my secure height; I shall not fall.
> My safety and glory are with God,
>   my strong rock and refuge.
> Trust God at all times, my people!
>   Pour out your hearts to God, our refuge!
> Mortals are a mere breath,
>   the powerful but an illusion. . . .
> Though wealth increase,
>   do not set your heart upon it.
> One thing God has said;
>   two things I have heard:
> Power belongs to God;
>   so too, LORD, does kindness,
> And you render to each of us
>   according to our deeds.

God alone is my rock and my salvation.

FROM PSALM 63

My soul clings fast to you;
your right hand upholds me.

> O God, you are my God—for you I long!
> For you my body yearns;
>   for you my soul thirsts,
> Like a land parched, lifeless,
>   and without water.
> So I look to you in the sanctuary
>   to see your power and glory.
> For your love is better than life;
>   my lips offer you worship!
> I will bless you as long as I live;
>   I will lift up my hands, calling
>   on your name. . . .
> When I think of you upon my bed,
>   through the night watches I will recall
> That you indeed are my help,
>   and in the shadow of your wings
>   I shout for joy.
> My soul clings fast to you;
>   your right hand upholds me. . . .

My soul clings fast to you;
your right hand upholds me.

FROM PSALM 65

May we be filled with the good things of your house.

> To you we owe our hymn of praise,
>   O God, on Zion;
> To you our vows must be fulfilled,
>   you who hear our prayers.
> To you all flesh must come
>   with its burden of wicked deeds.
> We are overcome by our sins;
>   only you can pardon them.
> Happy the chosen ones you bring
>   to dwell in your courts.
> May we be filled with the good things
>   of your house,
>   the blessings of your holy temple!
> You answer us with awesome deeds
>   of justice,
>   O God, our savior,
> The hope of all the ends of the earth,
>   and of far distant islands.
> You are robed in power,
>   you set up the mountains by
>   your might.
> You still the roaring of the seas,
>   the roaring of their waves,
>   the tumult of the peoples.

Distant peoples stand in awe of
  your marvels;
  east and west you make resound with joy.
You visit the earth and water it,
  you make it abundantly fertile.
God's stream is filled with water;
  with it you supply the world with grain.
Thus do you prepare the earth:
  you drench plowed furrows,
  and level their ridges.
With showers you keep the ground soft,
  blessing its young sprouts.
You adorn the year with your bounty;
  your paths drip with fruitful rain.
The untilled meadows also drip;
  the hills are robed with joy.
The pastures are clothed with flocks,
  the valleys blanketed with grain;
  they cheer and sing for joy.
May we be filled with the good things of your house.

FROM PSALM 66

Blessed be God, who did not refuse me
the kindness I sought in prayer.

> Shout joyfully to God, all you on earth;
>   sing of his glorious name;
>   give him glorious praise.
> Say to God: "How awesome your deeds!
>   Before your great strength
>   your enemies cringe.
> All on earth fall in worship before you;
>   they sing of you, sing of your name!"
> Come and see the works of God,
>   awesome in the deeds done for us.
> He changed the sea to dry land;
>   through the river they passed on foot.
> Therefore let us rejoice in him,
>   who rules by might forever,
> Whose eyes are fixed upon the nations.
>   Let no rebel rise to challenge!
> Bless our God, you peoples;
>   loudly sound his praise,
> Who has kept us alive
>   and not allowed our feet to slip.
> You tested us, O God,
>   tried us as silver tried by fire.
> You led us into a snare;

you bound us at the waist as captives.
You let captors set foot on our neck;
  we went through fire and water;
  then you led us out to freedom.
I will bring holocausts to your house;
  to you I will fulfill my vows,
The vows my lips pronounced
  and my mouth spoke in distress. . . .
Come and hear, all you who fear God,
  while I recount what has been done for me.
I called to the LORD with my mouth;
  praise was upon my tongue.
Had I cherished evil in my heart,
  the LORD would not have heard.
But God did hear and listened
  to my voice in prayer.
Blessed be God, who did not refuse me
  the kindness I sought in prayer.

Blessed be God, who did not refuse me
the kindness I sought in prayer.

From Psalm 67

May God's face shine upon us.

> May God be gracious to us and bless us;
>   may God's face shine upon us.
> So shall your rule be known upon the earth,
>   your saving power among all the nations.
> May the peoples praise you, God;
>   may all the peoples praise you!
> May the nations be glad and shout for joy;
>   for you govern the peoples justly,
>   you guide the nations upon the earth.
> May the peoples praise you, God;
>   may all the peoples praise you!
> The earth has yielded its harvest;
>   God, our God blesses us.
> May God bless us still;
>   that the ends of the earth
>   may revere our God.

May God's face shine upon us.

FROM PSALM 68

Our God is a God who saves.

> . . . .Sing to God, praise the divine name;
>   exalt the rider of the clouds.
> Rejoice before this God
>   whose name is the LORD.
> Father of the fatherless,
>   defender of widows—
>   this is the God whose abode is holy,
> Who gives a home to the forsaken,
>   who leads prisoners out to prosperity. . . .
> Blessed be the LORD day by day,
>   God, our salvation, who carries us.
> Our God is a God who saves;
>   escape from death is
>   in the LORD God's hands. . . .
> Summon again, O God, your power,
>   the divine power you once showed for us.
> Show it from your temple on behalf
>   of Jerusalem. . . .
> You kingdoms of the earth, sing to God;
>   chant the praises of the LORD,
> Who rides the heights of the ancient heavens,
>   whose voice is thunder, mighty thunder.
> Confess the power of God,
>   whose majesty protects Israel,

whose power is in the sky.
Awesome is God in his holy place,
the God of Israel,
who gives power and strength to his people.
Blessed be God!

Our God is a God who saves.

FROM PSALM 69

Answer me, LORD, in your generous love;
in your great mercy, turn to me.

> Save me, God,
>> for the waters have reached my neck.
> I have sunk into the mire of the deep,
>> where there is no foothold.
> I have gone down to the watery depths;
>> the flood overwhelms me.
> I am weary with crying out;
>> my throat is parched.
> My eyes have failed,
>> looking for my God. . . .
> God, you know my folly;
>> my faults are not hidden from you. . . .
> For your sake I bear insult,
>> shame covers my face.
> I have become an outcast to my kin,
>> a stranger to my mother's children. . . .
> They who sit at the gate gossip about me;
>> drunkards make me the butt of
>> their songs.
> But I pray to you, LORD,
>> for the time of your favor.
> God, in your great kindness, answer me
>> with your constant help.

Rescue me from the mire;
　do not let me sink.
Rescue me from my enemies
　and from the watery depths.
Do not let the floodwaters
　overwhelm me,
　nor the deep swallow me,
　nor the mouth of the pit close over me.
Answer me, LORD, in your generous love;
　in your great mercy, turn to me.
Do not hide your face from your servant;
　in my distress, hasten to answer me. . . .
You who know my reproach, my shame,
　my disgrace; before you stand all my foes.
Insult has broken my heart, and I am weak;
　I looked for compassion, but there was none,
　for comforters, but found none. . . .
I am afflicted and in pain;
　let your saving help protect me, God,
That I may praise God's name in song
　and glorify it with thanksgiving. . . .

Answer me, LORD, in your generous love;
in your great mercy turn to me.

From Psalm 70

You are my help and deliverer.
LORD, do not delay!

> Graciously rescue me, God!
>   Come quickly to help me, LORD!
> Confound and put to shame
>   those who seek my life.
> Turn back in disgrace
>   those who desire my ruin.
> Let those who say "Aha!"
>   turn back in their shame.
> But may all who seek you
>   rejoice and be glad in you.
> May those who long for your help
>   always say, "God be glorified!"
> Here I am, afflicted and poor.
>   God, come quickly!
> You are my help and deliverer.
>   LORD, do not delay!

You are my help and deliverer.
LORD, do not delay!

From Psalm 71

Be my rock and refuge, my secure stronghold.

> In you, LORD, I take refuge;
>> let me never be put to shame.
> In your justice rescue and deliver me;
>> listen to me and save me!
> Be my rock and refuge,
>> my secure stronghold;
>> for you are my rock and fortress.
> My God, rescue me from the power
>> of the wicked,
>> from the clutches of the violent.
> You are my hope, LORD;
>> my trust, God, from my youth.
> On you I depend since birth;
>> from my mother's womb you are my strength;
>> my hope in you never wavers. . . .
> You are my strong refuge!
> My mouth shall be filled with your praise,
>> shall sing your glory every day. . . .
> I will always hope in you
>> and add to all your praise.
> My mouth shall proclaim your just deeds,
>> day after day your acts of deliverance,
>> though I cannot number them all.
> I will speak of the mighty works of the LORD;

O God, I will tell
of your singular justice. . . .
You have done great things;
O God, who is your equal?
You have sent me many bitter afflictions,
but once more revive me.
From the watery depths of the earth
once more raise me up.
Restore my honor;
turn and comfort me. . . .
My lips will shout for joy as I sing
your praise;
my soul, too, which you have redeemed.
Yes, my tongue shall recount
your justice day by day. . . .

Be my rock and refuge, my secure stronghold.

FROM PSALM 73

God is the rock of my heart,
my portion forever.

> How good God is to the upright,
>   the LORD, to those who are clean of heart!
> But as for me, I lost my balance;
>   my feet all but slipped. . . .
> Since my heart was embittered
>   and my soul deeply wounded,
> I was stupid and could not understand;
>   I was like a brute beast in your presence.
> Yet I am always with you;
>   you take hold of my right hand.
> With your counsel you guide me,
>   and at the end receive me with honor.
> Whom else have I in the heavens?
>   None beside you delights me on earth.
> Though my flesh and my heart fail,
>   God is the rock of my heart, my portion
>   forever. . . .
> As for me, to be near God is my good,
>   to make the LORD God my refuge...

God is the rock of my heart,
my portion forever.

FROM PSALM 74

Do not forget forever the life of your afflicted.

> Why, God, have you cast us off forever?
> Why does your anger burn against
> the sheep of your pasture?
> Remember your flock that you gathered of old,
> the tribe you redeemed as your very own. . . .
> You, God, are my king from of old,
> winning victories throughout the earth.
> You stirred up the sea in your might. . . .
> You opened up springs and torrents,
> brought dry land out of
> the primeval waters.
> Yours the day and yours the night;
> you set the moon and sun in place.
> You fixed all the limits of the earth;
> summer and winter you made. . . .
> Do not surrender to beasts
> those who praise you;
> do not forget forever the life of
> your afflicted.
> Look to your covenant,
> for the land is filled with gloom. . . .
> Let not the oppressed turn back in shame;
> may the poor and needy praise your name. . . .

Do not forget forever the life of your afflicted.

FROM PSALM 75

We thank you, God, we give thanks.

> We thank you, God, we give thanks;
> we call upon your name,
> declare your wonderful deeds.
> You said: "I will choose the time;
> I will judge fairly.
> The earth and all its inhabitants
> will quake, but I have firmly
> set its pillars."
> So I say to the boastful: "Do not boast!"
> to the wicked: "Do not raise your horns!
> Do not raise your horns against heaven!
> Do not speak arrogantly against the Rock!"
> For judgment comes not from east
> or from west,
> not from the desert or from the mountains,
> But from God who decides,
> who brings some low
> and raises others high. . . .
> But I will rejoice forever;
> I will sing praise to the God of Jacob,
> Who has said: "I will break off
> all the horns of the wicked, but the horns
> of the just shall be lifted up."

We thank you, God, we give you thanks.

From Psalm 76

Make and keep vows to the LORD your God.

. . . .Terrible and awesome are you, [LORD],
 stronger than the ancient mountains.
Despoiled are the bold warriors;
 they sleep their final sleep;
 the hands of all the mighty have failed.
At your roar, O God of Jacob,
 chariots and steeds lay still.
So terrible and awesome are you;
 who can stand before you
 and your great anger?
From the heavens you pronounced sentence;
 the earth was terrified and reduced
 to silence,
When you arose, O God, for judgment
 to deliver the afflicted of the land. . . .
Make and keep vows to the LORD your God.
 May all present bring gifts to this
 awesome God,
Who checks the pride of princes,
 inspires awe among the kings of earth.

Make and keep vows to the LORD your God.

FROM PSALM 77

On the day of my distress I seek the LORD.

> I cry aloud to God,
>> cry to God to hear me.
>
> On the day of my distress I seek the LORD;
>> by night my hands are raised unceasingly;
>>
>> I refuse to be consoled.
>
> When I think of God, I groan;
>> as I ponder, my spirit grows faint.
>
> My eyes cannot close in sleep;
>> I am troubled and cannot speak.
>
> I consider the days of old;
>> the years long past I remember.
>
> In the night I meditate in my heart;
>> I ponder and my spirit broods:
>
> "Will the LORD reject us forever,
>> never again show favor;
>
> Has God's love ceased forever?
>> Has the promise failed for all ages?
>
> Has God forgotten mercy,
>> in anger withheld compassion?"
>
> I conclude: "My sorrow is this,
>> the right hand of the Most High has
>>
>> left us."
>
> I will remember the deeds of the LORD;
>> yes, your wonders of old I will remember.

I will recite all your works;
   your exploits I will tell.
Your way, O God, is holy;
   what God is as great as our God?
You alone are the God who did wonders;
   among the peoples you revealed your might.
With your arm you redeemed your people,
   the descendants of Jacob and Joseph.
The waters saw you, God;
   the waters saw you and lashed about,
   trembled even to their depths.
The clouds poured down their rains;
   the thunderheads rumbled;
   your arrows flashed back and forth.
The thunder of your chariot wheels resounded;
   your lightening lit up the world;
   the earth trembled and quaked.
Through the sea was your path;
   your way, through the mighty waters,
   though your footsteps were unseen.
You led your people like a flock
   under the care of Moses and Aaron.

On the day of my distress I seek the LORD.

From Psalm 79

May your compassion come quickly,
for we have been brought very low.

> . . . .We have become the reproach of
> our neighbors,
>> the scorn and derision of those around us.
> How long, LORD? Will you be angry forever?
>> Will your rage keep burning like fire?
>
> . . . .
>
> Do not hold past iniquities against us;
>> may your compassion come quickly,
>> for we have been brought very low.
> Help us, God our savior,
>> for the glory of your name.
> Deliver us, pardon our sins
>> for your name's sake. . . .
> Then we, your people, the sheep of
> your pasture,
>> will give thanks to you forever;
>> through all ages we will declare
>> your praise.

May your compassion come quickly,
for we have been brought very low.

FROM PSALM 80

O LORD of hosts, restore us.

> Shepherd of Israel, listen,
>   guide of the flock of Joseph!
> From your throne upon the cherubim
>   reveal yourself
>   to Ephraim, Benjamin, and Manasseh.
> Stir up your power, come to save us.
>   O LORD of hosts, restore us;
>   let your face shine upon us,
>   that we may be saved.
> LORD of hosts,
>   how long will you burn with anger
>   while your people pray?
> You have fed them the bread of tears,
>   made them drink tears in abundance.
> You have left us to be fought over
>   by our neighbors;
>   our enemies deride us.
> O LORD of hosts, restore us;
>   let your face shine upon us,
>   that we may be saved.
> You brought a vine out of Egypt;
>   you drove away the nations and planted it.
> You cleared the ground;
>   it took root and filled the land.

The mountains were covered by its shadow,
  the cedars of God by its branches.
It sent out boughs as far as the sea,
  shoots as far as the river.
Why have you broken down the walls,
  so that all who pass by pluck its fruit?
The boar from the forest strips the vine;
  the beast of the field feeds upon it.
Turn again, Lord of hosts;
  look down from heaven and see;
Attend to this vine,
  the shoot your right hand has planted. . . .
Lord of hosts, restore us;
  let your face shine upon us,
  that we may be saved.

O Lord of hosts, restore us.

FROM PSALM 83

God, be not still and unmoved.

> God, do not be silent;
>> God, be not still and unmoved!
> See how your enemies rage. . . .
> Show them you alone are the LORD,
>> the Most High over all the earth.

God, be not still and unmoved.

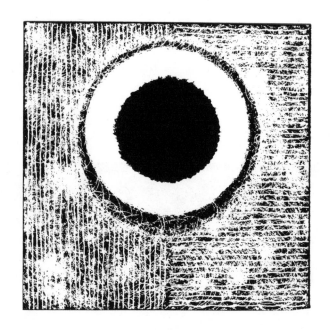

From Psalm 84

O LORD of hosts,
happy are those who trust in you.

How lovely your dwelling, O LORD of hosts!
My soul yearns and pines
for the courts of the LORD.
My heart and flesh cry out
for the living God.
As the sparrow finds a home
and the swallow a nest to settle her young,
My home is by your altars,
LORD of hosts, my king and my God!
Happy are those who dwell in your house!
They never cease to praise you.
Happy are those who find refuge in you,
whose hearts are set on pilgrim roads.
As they pass through the Baca Valley,
they find spring water to drink.
Also from pools the LORD provides water
for those who lose their way.
They pass through outer and inner walls
and see the God of gods on Zion.
LORD of hosts, hear my prayer;
listen, God of Jacob.
O God, look kindly on our shield;
look upon the face of your anointed.

Better one day in your courts
  than a thousand elsewhere.
Better the threshold of the house of my God
  than a home in the tents of the wicked.
For a sun and shield is the LORD God,
  bestowing all grace and glory.
The LORD withholds no good thing
  from those who walk without reproach.
O LORD of hosts,
  happy are those who trust in you!

O LORD of hosts,
happy are those who trust in you.

Better the
threshold
of the house
of my God,

than a home
in the tents
of the wicked.

From Psalm 85

Show us, LORD, your love.

> . . . .Restore us once more, God, our savior;
>   abandon your wrath against us.
> Will you be angry with us forever,
>   drag out your anger for all generations?
> Please give us life again,
>   that your people may rejoice in you.
> Show us, LORD, your love;
>   grant us your salvation.
> I will listen for the word of God;
>   surely the LORD will proclaim peace
> To his people, to the faithful,
>   to those who trust in him.
> Near indeed is salvation for the loyal;
>   prosperity will fill our land. . . .
> The LORD will surely grant abundance;
>   our land will yield its increase.
> Prosperity will march before the LORD,
>   and good fortune will follow behind.

Show us, LORD, your love.

FROM PSALM 86

LORD, hear my prayer;
listen to my cry for help.

> Hear me, LORD, and answer me,
>> for I am poor and oppressed.
>
> Preserve my life, for I am loyal;
>> save your servant who trusts in you.
>
> You are my God; pity me, LORD;
>> to you I call all the day.
>
> Gladden the soul of your servant;
>> to you, LORD, I lift up my soul.
>
> LORD, you are kind and forgiving,
>> most loving to all who call on you.
>
> LORD, hear my prayer;
>> listen to my cry for help.
>
> In this time of trouble I call,
>> for you will answer me. . . .
>
> For you are great and do wondrous deeds;
>> and you alone are God.
>
> Teach me, LORD, your way
>> that I may walk in your truth,
>> singlehearted and revering your name.
>
> I will praise you with all my heart,
>> glorify your name forever, LORD, my God.
>
> Your love for me is great. . . .
>
> Turn to me, have pity on me;

give your strength to your servant;
save this child of your handmaid.
Give me a sign of your favor:
make my enemies see, to their confusion,
that you, LORD, help and comfort me.

LORD, hear my prayer;
listen to my cry for help,

FROM PSALM 88

All day I call on you, LORD;
I stretch out my hands to you.

> LORD, my God, I call out by day;
>   at night I cry aloud in your presence.
> Let my prayer come before you;
>   incline your ear to my cry.
> For my soul is filled with troubles;
>   my life draws near to Sheol.
> I am reckoned with those who go
>   down to the pit;
> I am weak, without strength. . . .
> All day I call on you, LORD;
>   I stretch out my hands to you. . . .
> I cry out to you, LORD;
>   in the morning my prayer comes before you.
> Why do you reject me, LORD?
>   Why hide your face from me?
>
>   . . . .
>
> Because of you, companions shun me;
>   my only friend is darkness.

All day I call on you, LORD;
I stretch out my hands to you.

From Psalm 89

Truly the LORD is our shield.

> The promises of the LORD I will sing forever,
> proclaim your loyalty through all ages.
> For you said, "My love is established
> forever; my loyalty will stand
> as long as the heavens."
>
> . . . .
>
> Yours are the heavens, yours the earth;
> you founded the world
> and everything in it. . . .
> Mighty your arm, strong your hand,
> your right hand is ever exalted.
> Justice and judgment are the foundation
> of your throne;
> love and loyalty march before you.
> Happy the people who know you, LORD,
> who walk in the radiance of your face.
> In your name they sing joyfully all the day;
> at your victory they raise
> the festal shout.
> You are their majestic strength;
> by your favor our horn is exalted.
> Truly the LORD is our shield,
> the Holy One of Israel our king!
>
> . . . .
>
> Remember how brief is my life,

how frail the race you created!
What mortal can live and not see death?
Who can escape the power of Sheol?
Where are your promises of old, Lord,
the loyalty sworn to David?

Truly the Lord is our shield.

FROM PSALM 90

May the favor of the LORD our God be ours.

> LORD, you have been our refuge
> through all generations.
> Before the mountains were born,
> the earth and the world brought forth,
> from eternity to eternity you are God.
> A thousand years in your eyes
> are merely a yesterday,
> But humans you return to dust. . . .
> They disappear like sleep at dawn;
> they are like grass that dies.
> It sprouts green in the morning;
> by evening it is dry and withered. . . .
> Our life ebbs away under your wrath;
> our years end like a sigh.
> Seventy is the sum of our years,
> or eighty, if we are strong;
> Most of them are sorrow and toil;
> they pass quickly, we are all but gone. . . .
> Teach us to count our days aright,
> that we may gain wisdom of heart.
> Relent, O LORD! How long?
> Have pity on your servants!
> Fill us at daybreak with your love,
> that all our days we may sing for joy.

Make us glad as many days
  as you humbled us,
    for as many years as we have seen trouble.
Show your deeds to your servants,
  your glory to their children.
May the favor of the LORD our God be ours.
  Prosper the work of our hands!
  Prosper the work of our hands!

May the favor of the LORD our God be ours.

FROM PSALM 91

God's faithfulness is a protecting shield.

You who dwell in the shelter of
the Most High,
who abide in the shadow of the Almighty,
Say to the LORD, "My refuge and fortress,
my God in whom I trust."
God will rescue you from
the fowler's snare,
from the destroying plague,
Will shelter you with pinions,
spread wings that you may take refuge;
God's faithfulness is a protecting shield.
You shall not fear the terror of the night
nor the arrow that flies by day,
Nor the pestilence that roams in darkness,
nor the plague that ravishes at noon.
Though a thousand fall at your side,
ten thousand at your right hand,
near you it shall not come. . . .
You have the LORD for your refuge;
you have made the Most High
your stronghold.
No evil shall befall you,
no affliction come near your tent.
For God commands the angels

to guard you in all your ways.
With their hands they shall support you,
   lest you strike your foot
   against a stone. . . .
Whoever clings to me I will deliver;
   whoever knows my name I will set on high.
All who call upon me I will answer;
   I will be with them in distress;
   I will deliver them and give them honor.
With length of days I will satisfy them
   and show them my saving power.

God's faithfulness is a protecting shield.

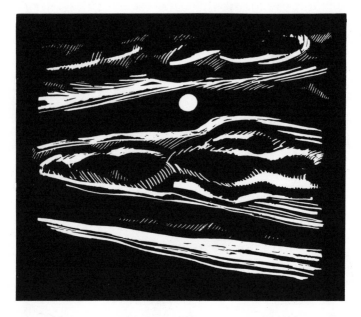

FROM PSALM 92

How great are your works, LORD!
How profound your purpose!

It is good to give thanks to the LORD,
    to sing praise to your name, Most High,
To acclaim your love in the morning,
    your faithfulness in the night. . . .
For you make me jubilant, LORD,
    by your deeds; at the work of your hands
    I shout for joy.
How great are your works, LORD!
    How profound your purpose! . . . .
You have given me the strength of
    a wild bull;
    you have poured rich oil upon me. . . .
The just shall flourish like the palm tree,
    shall grow like a cedar of Lebanon.
Planted in the house of the LORD,
    they shall flourish in the courts
    of our God.
They shall bear fruit even in old age,
    always vigorous and sturdy,
As they proclaim: "The LORD is just;
    our rock, in whom there is no wrong."

How great are your works, LORD!
How profound your purpose!

FROM PSALM 93

Powerful in the heavens is the LORD.

> The LORD is king, robed with majesty;
> the LORD is robed, girdled with might.
> The world will surely stand in place,
> never to be moved.
> Your throne stands firm from of old;
> you are from everlasting, LORD.
> The flood has raised up, LORD;
> the flood has raised up its roar;
> the flood has raised its pounding waves.
> More powerful than the roar of many waters,
> more powerful than the breakers of the sea,
> powerful in the heavens is the LORD.
> Your decrees are firmly established;
> holiness belongs to your house, LORD,
> for all the length of days.

Powerful in the heavens is the LORD.

FROM PSALM 94

When cares increase within me,
your comfort gives me joy.

> LORD, avenging God,
>> avenging God, shine forth!
>
> Rise up, judge of the earth;
>> give the proud what they deserve.
>
> How long, LORD, shall the wicked,
>> how long shall the wicked glory?
>
> Does the one who shaped the ear not hear?
>> The one who formed the eye not see?
>
> Does the one who guides nations
>> not rebuke?
>> The one who teaches humans
>> not have knowledge?
>
> The LORD does know human plans;
>> they are only puffs of air.
>
> Happy those whom you guide, LORD,
>> whom you teach by your instruction. . . .
>
> You, LORD, will not forsake your people,
>> nor abandon your very own. . . .
>
> Who will rise up for me against the wicked?
>> Who will stand up for me against evildoers?
>
> If the LORD were not my help,
>> I would long have been silent in the grave.
>
> When I say, "My foot is slipping,"

your love, LORD, holds me up.
When cares increase within me,
your comfort gives me joy. . . .

When cares increase within me,
your comfort gives me joy.

From Psalm 95

Come, let us sing joyfully to the LORD.

> Come, let us sing joyfully to the LORD;
>   cry out to the rock of our salvation.
> Let us greet him with a song of praise,
>   joyfully sing out our psalms.
> For the LORD is the great God,
>   the great king over all gods,
> Whose hand holds the depths of the earth,
>   who owns the tops of the mountains.
> The sea and dry land belong to God,
>   who made them, formed them by hand.
> Enter, let us bow down in worship;
>   let us kneel before the LORD
>   who made us,
> For this is our God,
>   whose people we are,
>   God's well-tended flock. . . .

Come, let us sing joyfully to the LORD.

FROM PSALM 96

For great is the LORD and highly to be praised.

> Sing to the LORD a new song;
>   sing to the LORD, all the earth.
> Sing to the LORD, bless his name;
>   announce his salvation day after day.
> Tell God's glory among the nations;
>   among all peoples, God's marvelous deeds.
> For great is the LORD
>   and highly to be praised,
>   to be feared above all gods.
> For the gods of the nations all do nothing,
>   but the LORD made the heavens.
> Splendor and power go before him;
>   power and grandeur are in his holy place.
> Give to the LORD, you families of nations,
>   give to the LORD glory and might;
>   give to the LORD the glory due his name!
> Bring gifts and enter his courts;
>   bow down to the LORD, splendid in holiness.
> Tremble before God, all the earth;
>   say among the nations: The LORD is king.
> The world will surely stand fast,
>   never to be moved.
>   God rules the peoples with fairness.
> Let the heavens be glad

and the earth rejoice;
let the sea and what fills it resound;
let the plains be joyful and all
that is in them.
Then let all the trees of the forest rejoice
before the LORD who comes,
who comes to govern the earth,
To govern the world with justice
and the peoples with faithfulness.

For great is the LORD and highly to be praised.

FROM PSALM 97

The LORD . . . protects the lives of the faithful.

> The LORD is king; let the earth rejoice;
>   let the many islands be glad.
> Clouds and darkness surround the LORD;
>   justice and right are the foundation
>   of his throne.
> Fire goes before him;
>   everywhere it consumes the foes.
> Lightening illumines the world;
>   the earth sees and trembles.
> The mountains melt like wax before the LORD,
>   before the LORD of all the earth.
> The heavens proclaim God's justice;
>   all peoples see his glory.
> All who serve idols are put to shame,
>   who glory in worthless things;
>   all gods bow down before you.
> Zion hears and is glad,
>   and the cities of Judah rejoice
>   because of your judgments, O LORD.
> You, LORD, are the most high
>   over all the earth,
>   exalted far above all gods.
> The LORD loves those who hate evil,
>   protects the lives of the faithful,

rescues them from the hand of the wicked.
Light dawns for the just;
　gladness for the honest of heart.
Rejoice in the LORD, you just,
　and praise his holy name.

The LORD . . . protects the lives of the faithful.

From Psalm 98

All the ends of the earth have seen
the victory of our God.

> Sing a new song to the LORD,
>   who has done marvelous deeds,
> Whose right hand and holy arm
>   have won the victory.
> The LORD has made his victory known;
>   has revealed his triumph for the
>   nations to see,
> Has remembered faithful love
>   toward the house of Israel.
> All the ends of the earth have seen
>   the victory of our God. . . .
> With trumpets and the sound of the horn
>   shout with joy to the king, the LORD.
> Let the sea and what fills it resound,
>   the world and those who dwell there.
> Let the rivers clap their hands,
>   the mountains shout with them for joy,
> Before the LORD who comes,
>   who comes to govern the earth,
> To govern the world with justice
>   and the peoples with fairness.

All the ends of the earth have seen
the victory of our God.

FROM PSALM 99

O [LORD], lover of justice,
you alone have established fairness.

> . . . .The LORD is great on Zion,
> exalted above all the peoples.
> Let them praise your great and awesome name:
> Holy is God!
> O mighty king, lover of justice,
> you alone have established fairness;
> you have created just rule. . . .
> Exalt the LORD, our God;
> bow down before his footstool;
> holy is God!
> Moses and Aaron were among his priests,
> Samuel among those who called
> on God's name;
> they called on the LORD, who answered them.
> From the pillar of cloud God spoke to them;
> they kept the decrees, the law
> they received.
> O LORD, our God, you answered them;
> you were a forgiving God,
> though you punished their offenses. . . .

O [LORD], lover of justice,
you alone have established fairness.

From Psalm 100

Good indeed is the LORD . . .
whose faithfulness lasts through every age.

> Shout joyfully to the LORD, all you lands;
>> worship the LORD with cries of gladness;
>> come before him with joyful song.
>
> Know that the LORD is God,
>> our maker to whom we belong,
>> whose people we are,
>> God's well-tended flock.
>
> Enter the temple gates with praise.
>> its courts with thanksgiving.
>
> Give thanks to God, bless his name;
>> good indeed is the LORD,
>
> Whose love endures forever,
>> whose faithfulness lasts through every age.

Good indeed is the LORD . . .
whose faithfulness lasts through every age.

FROM PSALM 101

I follow the way of integrity,
when will you come to me?

> **I sing of love and justice;**
> **to you, LORD, I sing praise.**
> **I follow the way of integrity;**
> **when will you come to me?**
> **I act with integrity of heart. . . .**

I follow the way of integrity,
when will you come to me?

From Psalm 102

Turn your ear to me;
when I call, answer me quickly.

> Lord, hear my prayer;
>   let my cry come to you.
> Do not hide your face from me
>   now that I am in distress.
> Turn your ear to me;
>   when I call, answer me quickly.
> For my days vanish like smoke;
>   my bones burn away as in a furnace.
> I am withered, dried up like grass,
>   too wasted to eat my food.
> From my loud groaning
>   I become just skin and bones.
> I am like a desert owl,
>   like an owl among the ruins.
> I lie awake and moan,
>   like a lone sparrow on the roof. . . .
> I eat ashes like bread,
>   mingle my drink with tears. . . .
> My days are like a lengthening shadow;
>   I wither like the grass.
> But you, Lord, are enthroned forever;
>   your renown is for all generations.
> You will again show mercy to Zion;

now is the time for pity;

the appointed time has come. . . .

God has shattered my strength in mid-course,

has cut short my days.

I plead, O my God,

do not take me in the midst of my days.

Your years last through all generations.

Of old you laid the earth's foundations;

the heavens are the work of your hands.

They perish, but you remain;

they all wear out like a garment;

Like clothing you change them

and they are changed,

but you are the same,

your years have no end.

May the children of your servants live on;

may their descendants live

in your presence.

Turn your ear to me;
when I call, answer me quickly.

FROM PSALM 103

Merciful and gracious is the LORD;
slow to anger, abounding in kindness.

> Bless the LORD, my soul;
>   all my being, bless his holy name!
> Bless the LORD, my soul;
>   do not forget all the gifts of God,
> Who pardons all your sins,
>   heals all your ills,
> Delivers your life from the pit,
>   surrounds you with love and compassion,
> Fills your days with good things;
>   your youth is renewed like the eagle's.
> The LORD does righteous deeds,
>   brings justice to all the oppressed.
> His ways were revealed to Moses,
>   mighty deeds to the people of Israel.
> Merciful and gracious is the LORD,
>   slow to anger, abounding in kindness.
> God does not always rebuke,
>   nurses no lasting anger,
> Has not dealt with us as our sins merit,
>   nor requited us as our deeds deserve.
> As the heavens tower over the earth,
>   so God's love towers over the faithful.
> As far as the east is from the west,

so far have our sins been removed from us.
As a father has compassion on his children,
  so the LORD has compassion on the faithful.
For he knows how we are formed,
  remembers that we are dust.
Our days are like the grass;
  like flowers of the field we blossom.
The wind sweeps over us and we are gone;
  our place knows us no more.
But the LORD's kindness is forever
  toward the faithful from age to age. . . .
Bless the LORD, all creatures,
  everywhere in God's domain.
Bless the LORD, my soul!

Merciful and gracious is the LORD,
slow to anger, abounding in kindness.

From Psalm 104

[Lord], you renew the face of the earth.

> Bless the Lord, my soul!
>> Lord, my God, you are great indeed!

. . . .

> You spread out the heavens like a tent. . . .
> You make the clouds your chariot;
>> you travel on the wings of the wind.
> You make the winds your messengers,
>> flaming fire, your ministers.
> You fixed the earth on its foundation,
>> never to be moved.
> The ocean covered it like a garment;
>> above the mountains stood the waters.
> At your roar they took flight;
>> at the sound of your thunder they fled. . . .
> You made springs flow into channels
>> that wind among the mountains.
> They give drink to every beast
>> of the field. . . .
> You water the mountains from your palace;
>> by your labor the earth abounds.
> You raise grass for the cattle
>> and plants for our beasts of burden.
> You bring bread from the earth,
>> and wine to gladden our hearts,

Oil to make our faces gleam,
  food to build our strength. . . .
You made the moon to mark the seasons,
  the sun that knows the hour of its setting.
You bring darkness and night falls,
  then all the beasts of the forest
  roam abroad.
Young lions roar for prey;
  they seek their food from God.
When the sun rises, they steal away
  and rest in their dens.
People go forth to their work,
  to their labor till evening falls.
How varied are your works, LORD!
  In wisdom, you have wrought them all;
  the earth is full of your creatures. . . .
All of them look to you
  to give them food in due time.
When you give to them they gather;
  when you open your hand
  they are well filled.
When you hide your face, they are lost.
  When you take away their breath,
  they perish and return to the dust
  from which they came.
When you send forth your breath,
  they are created,

and you renew the face of the earth.
May the glory of the LORD endure forever;
   may the LORD be glad in these works!

      . . . .

I will sing to the LORD all my life;
   I will sing praise to my God
   while I live.
May my theme be pleasing to God;
   I will rejoice in the LORD. . . .

[LORD], you renew the face of the earth.

FROM PSALM 105

Rely on the mighty LORD,
constantly seek his face.

> Give thanks to the LORD, invoke his name;
> make known among the peoples his deeds!
>
> . . . .
>
> Rely on the mighty LORD;
> constantly seek his face.
> Recall the wondrous deeds he has done,
> his signs and his words of judgment. . . .
> The LORD is our God
> who rules the whole earth.
> He remembers forever his covenant,
> the pact imposed for
> a thousand generations. . . .
> For he remembered his sacred word
> to Abraham his servant.
> He brought his people out with joy,
> his chosen ones with shouts of triumph.
> He gave them the lands of the nations,
> the wealth of the peoples to own,
> That they might keep his laws
> and observe his teachings.

Rely on the mighty LORD;
constantly seek his face.

FROM PSALM 106

Remember me, LORD . . .
come to me with your saving help.

> Give thanks to the LORD, who is good,
>   whose love endures forever.
> Who can tell the mighty deeds of the LORD,
>   proclaim in full God's praise?
> Happy those who do what is right,
>   whose deeds are always just.
> Remember me, LORD, as you favor your people;
>   come to me with your saving help.
> That I may see the prosperity of your chosen,
>   rejoice in the joy of your people,
>   and glory with your heritage. . . .
> Save us, LORD, our God;
>   gather us from among the nations
> That we may give thanks to your holy name
>   and glory in praising you.
> Blessed be the LORD, the God of Israel,
>   from everlasting to everlasting!
>   Let all the people say, Amen!

Remember me, LORD . . .
come to me with your saving help.

From Psalm 107

Whoever is wise . . . will ponder
the merciful deeds of the LORD.

"Give thanks to the LORD who is good,
  whose love endures forever!"
Let that be the prayer
  of the LORD's redeemed,
    those redeemed from the hand of the foe. . . .
Some had lost their way in a barren desert;
  found no path toward a city to live in.
They were hungry and thirsty;
  their life was ebbing away.
In their distress they cried to the LORD,
  who rescued them in their peril,
Guided them by a direct path
  so they reached a city to live in.
Let them thank the LORD for such kindness,
  such wondrous deeds for mere mortals.
For he satisfied the thirsty,
  filled the hungry with good things.
Some lived in darkness and gloom,
  in prison, bound with chains. . . .
    they stumbled with no one to help.
In their distress they cried to the LORD,
  who saved them in their peril,
Led them forth from the darkness and gloom

and broke their chains asunder.
Let them thank the LORD for such kindness,
    such wondrous deeds for mere mortals.
For he broke down the gates of bronze
    and snapped the bars of iron.
Some fell sick. . . .
In their distress they cried to the LORD,
    who saved them in their peril,
Sent forth the word to heal them,
    snatched them from the grave.
Let them thank the LORD for such kindness,
    such wondrous deeds for mere mortals.
Let them offer a sacrifice in thanks,
    declare his works with shouts of joy.
Some went off to sea in ships,
    plied their trade on the deep waters.
They saw the works of the LORD,
    the wonders of God in the deep.
He spoke and roused a storm wind;
    it tossed the waves on high.
They rose up to the heavens,
    sank to the depths;
    their hearts trembled at the danger.
They reeled, staggered like drunkards;
    their skill was of no avail.
In their distress they cried to the LORD,
    who brought them out of their peril,

Hushed the storm to a murmur;
   the waves of the sea were stilled.
They rejoiced that the sea grew calm,
   that God brought them to the harbor
   they longed for.
Let them thank the LORD for such kindness,
   such wondrous deeds for mere mortals.
Let them praise him
   in the assembly of the people, give thanks in
the council of the elders. . . .
Whoever is wise will take note
   of these things,
   will ponder the merciful deeds of the LORD.

Whoever is wise . . . will ponder
the merciful deeds of the LORD.

FROM PSALM 108

For your love, [Lord], towers to the heavens,
your faithfulness to the skies.

> **My heart is steadfast, God;**
> **my heart is steadfast.**
> **I will sing and chant praise. . . .**
> **I will praise you among the peoples, Lord;**
> **I will chant your praise among the nations.**
> **For your love towers to the heavens;**
> **your faithfulness to the skies.**
> **Appear on high over the heavens, God;**
> **may your glory appear above all the earth.**
> **Help with your right hand and answer us,**
> **that your loved ones may escape. . . .**

For your love, [Lord], towers to the heavens,
your faithfulness to the skies.

FROM PSALM 109

Help me, LORD, my God;
save me in your kindness.

> O God, whom I praise, do not be silent,
>   for wicked and treacherous mouths
>   attack me.
> They speak against me with lying tongues;
>   with hateful words they surround me,
>   attacking me without cause.
> In return for my love they slander me,
>   even though I prayed for them.
> They repay me evil for good. . . .
> But you, LORD, my God,
>   deal kindly with me for your name's sake;
>   in your great mercy, rescue me.
> For I am sorely in need;
>   my heart is pierced within me.
> Like a lengthening shadow I near my end. . . .
> Help me, LORD, my God;
>   save me in your kindness. . . .
> I will give fervent thanks to the LORD;
>   before all I will praise my God.
> For God stands at the right hand of the poor
>   to defend them against unjust accusers.

Help me, LORD, my God;
save me in your kindness.

FROM PSALM 111

The fear of the LORD
is the beginning of wisdom.

> I will praise the LORD with all my heart
>   in the assembled congregation. . . .
> Great are the works of the LORD,
>   to be treasured for all their delights.
> Majestic and glorious is your work,
>   your wise design endures forever.
> You won renown for your wondrous deeds;
>   gracious and merciful is the LORD.
> You gave food to those who fear you,
>   mindful of your covenant forever.
> You showed powerful deeds to your people. . . .
> The works of your hands are right and true,
>   reliable all your decrees,
> Established forever and ever,
>   to be observed with loyalty and care.
> You sent deliverance to your people,
>   ratified your covenant forever;
>   holy and awesome is your name.
> The fear of the LORD
>   is the beginning of wisdom;
>   prudent are all who live by it.

The fear of the LORD
is the beginning of wisdom.

From Psalm 112

Their hearts are steadfast, trusting the LORD.

> Happy are those who fear the LORD,
>> who greatly delight in God's commands.
>
> Their descendants shall be mighty
>> in the land,
>>
>> a generation upright and blessed.
>
> Wealth and riches shall be in their homes;
>> their prosperity shall endure forever.
>
> They shine through the darkness,
>> a light for the upright;
>>
>> they are gracious, merciful and just.
>
> All goes well for those gracious in lending,
>> who conduct their affairs with justice.
>
> They shall never be shaken;
>> the just shall be remembered forever.
>
> They shall not fear an ill report;
>> their hearts are steadfast,
>>
>> trusting the LORD.
>
> Their hearts are tranquil, without fear,
>> till at last they look down on their foes.
>
> Lavishly they give to the poor;
>> their prosperity shall endure forever,
>>
>> their horn shall be exalted in honor. . . .

The fear of the LORD is the beginning of wisdom.

FROM PSALM 113

The LORD raises the needy from the dust.

> Praise, you servants of the LORD,
>   praise the name of the LORD.
> Blessed be the name of the LORD
>   both now and forever.
> From the rising of the sun to its setting
>   let the name of the LORD be praised.
> High above all nations is the LORD;
>   above the heavens God's glory.
> Who is like the LORD,
>   our God enthroned on high,
>   looking down on heaven and earth?
> The LORD raises the needy from the dust,
>   lifts the poor from the ash heap,
> Seats them with princes,
>   the princes of the people. . . .

The LORD raises the needy from the dust.

FROM PSALM 115

Whatever God wills is done.

> Not to us, LORD, not to us
>   but to your name give glory
>   because of your faithfulness and love.
> Why should the nations say,
>   "Where is their God?"
> Our God is in heaven;
>   whatever God wills is done. . . .
> The house of Israel trusts in the LORD,
>   who is their help and their shield.
> The house of Aaron trusts in the LORD,
>   who is their help and shield.
> Those who fear the LORD trust in the LORD,
>   who is their help and shield.
> The LORD remembers us and will bless us,
>   will bless the house of Israel,
>   will bless the house of Aaron,
> Will bless those who fear the LORD,
>   small and great alike. . . .

Whatever God wills is done.

FROM PSALM 116

O LORD, save my life!

> I love the LORD, who listened
>   to my voice in supplication,
> Who turned an ear to me
>   on the day I called.
> I was caught by the cords of death;
>   the snares of Sheol had seized me;
>   I felt agony and dread.
> Then I called on the name of the LORD,
>   "O LORD, save my life!"
> Gracious is the LORD and just;
>   yes, our God is merciful.
> The LORD protects the simple;
>   I was helpless, but God saved me.
> Return, my soul, to your rest;
>   The LORD has been good to you.
> For my soul has been freed from death,
>   my eyes from tears, my feet from stumbling.
> I shall walk before the LORD
>   in the land of the living.
> I kept faith, even when I said,
>   "I am greatly afflicted!"
> I said in my alarm,
>   "No one can be trusted!"
> How can I repay the LORD

for all the good done for me?
I will raise the cup of salvation
  and call on the name of the LORD.
I will pay my vows to the LORD
  in the presence of all his people.
Too costly in the eyes of the LORD
  is the death of his faithful.
LORD, I am your servant . . .
  you have loosed my bonds.
I will offer a sacrifice of thanksgiving
  and call on the name of the LORD.
I will pay my vows to the LORD
  in the presence of all his people. . . .

O LORD, save my life!

FROM PSALM 117

The LORD's love for us is strong.

> **Praise the LORD, all you nations!**
> **Give glory, all you peoples!**
> **The LORD's love for us is strong;**
> **the LORD is faithful forever.**

The LORD's love for us is strong.

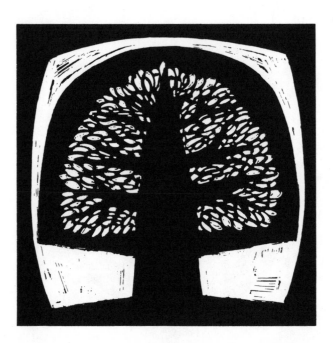

From Psalm 118

I was hard pressed and falling,
but the LORD came to my help.

> Give thanks to the LORD, who is good,
>   whose love endures forever.
> Let the house of Israel say,
>   God's love endures forever.
> Let the house of Aaron say,
>   God's love endures forever.
> Let those who fear the LORD say,
>   God's love endures forever.
> In danger I called on the LORD;
>   the LORD answered me and set me free.
> The LORD is with me; I am not afraid;
>   what can mortals do against me?
> The LORD is with me as my helper;
>   I shall look in triumph on my foes.
> Better to take refuge in the LORD
>   than to put one's trust in mortals.
> Better to take refuge in the LORD
>   than to put one's trust in princes. . . .
> I was hard pressed and falling,
>   but the LORD came to my help.
> The LORD, my strength and might,
>   came to me as savior.
> The joyful shout of deliverance

is heard in the tents of the victors:
"The LORD's right hand strikes with power;
the LORD's right hand is raised;
the LORD's right hand strikes with power."
I shall not die but live
and declare the deeds of the LORD.
The LORD chastised me harshly,
but did not hand me over to death. . . .
You are my God, I give you thanks;
my God, I offer you praise.
Give thanks to the LORD, who is good,
whose love endures forever.

I was hard pressed and falling,
but the LORD came to my help.

FROM PSALM 119

My soul longs for your salvation;
I put my hope in your word.
       . . . .With all my heart I seek you, [LORD];
          do not let me stray from your commands.
       In my heart I treasure your promise,
          that I may not sin against you.
       Blessed are you, O LORD;
          teach me your laws. . . .
       I will ponder your precepts
          and consider your paths.
       In your laws I take delight;
          I will never forget your word.
       Be kind to your servant that I may live,
          that I may keep your word.
       Open my eyes to see clearly
          the wonders of your teachings.
       I am a sojourner in the land;
          do not hide your commands from me.
       At all times my soul is stirred
          with longing for your edicts. . . .
       Free me from disgrace and contempt,
          for I observe your decrees. . . .
       Your decrees are my delight;
          they are my counselors.
       I lie prostrate in the dust;

give me life in accord with your word.
I disclosed my ways and you answered me;
  teach me your laws.
Make me understand the way of your precepts;
  I will ponder your wondrous deeds.
I weep in bitter pain,
  in accord with your word to strengthen me.
Lead me from the way of deceit;
  favor me with your teaching.
The way of loyalty I have chosen;
  I have set your edicts before me.
I cling to your decrees, LORD;
  do not let me come to shame.
I will run the way of your commands,
  for you open my docile heart. . . .
Give me insight to observe your teaching,
  to keep it with all my heart. . . .
Let your love come to me, LORD,
  salvation in accord with your promise.
Let me answer my taunters with a word,
  for I trust in your word. . . .
Remember your word to your servant
  by which you give me hope.
This is my comfort in affliction,
  your promise that gives me life. . . .
My portion is the LORD;
  I promise to keep your words.

I entreat you with all my heart; have mercy
   on me in accord with your promise. . . .
You have treated your servant well,
   according to your word, O LORD.
Teach me wisdom and knowledge,
   for in your commands I trust. . . .
It was good for me to be afflicted,
   in order to learn your laws.
Teaching from your lips
   is more precious to me
   than heaps of silver and gold.
Your hands made me and fashioned me;
   give me insight to learn your commands. . . .
I know, LORD, that your edicts are just;
   though you afflict me, you are faithful.
May your love comfort me
   in accord with your promise
   to your servant.
Show me compassion that I may live,
   for your teaching is my delight. . . .
My soul longs for your salvation;
   I put my hope in your word.
My eyes long to see your promise.
   When will you comfort me?
I am like a wineskin shriveled by smoke,
   but I have not forgotten your laws,
   how long can your servant survive?. . . .

All your commands are steadfast.

   Help me! I am pursued without cause.

They have almost ended my life on earth,

   but I do not forsake your precepts.

In your kindness give me life,

   to keep the decrees you have spoken.

Your word, LORD, stands forever;

   it is firm as the heavens.

Through all generations your truth endures;

   fixed to stand firm like the earth. . . .

I will never forget your precepts;

   through them you give me life.

I am yours; save me,

   for I cherish your precepts. . . .

Your word is a lamp for my feet,

   a light for my path.

I make a solemn vow

   to keep your just edicts.

I am very much afflicted, LORD;

   give me life in accord with your word. . . .

My life is always at risk,

   but I do not forget your teaching. . . .

You are my refuge and shield;

   in your word I hope. . . .

Sustain me by your promise that I may live;

   do not disappoint me in my hope.

Strengthen me that I may be safe,

ever to contemplate your laws. . . .
Guarantee your servant's welfare;
  do not let the arrogant oppress me.
My eyes long to see your salvation
  and the justice of your promise.
Act with kindness toward your servant;
  teach me your laws.
I am your servant; give me discernment
  that I may know your decrees.
It is time for the LORD to act. . . .
Turn to me and be gracious,
  your edict for lovers of your name.
Steady my feet in accord with your promise;
  do not let iniquity lead me.
Free me from human oppression,
  that I may keep your precepts.
Let your face shine upon your servant;
  teach me your laws.
My eyes shed streams of tears
  because your teaching is not followed. . . .
Though distress and anguish come upon me,
  your commands are my delight.
Your decrees are forever just;
  give me discernment that I may live. . . .
I rise before dawn and cry out;
  I put my hope in your words.
My eyes greet the night watches

as I meditate on your promise.
Hear my voice in your love, O LORD;
    by your edict give me life. . . .
Look at my affliction and rescue me,
    for I have not forgotten your teaching.
Take up my cause and redeem me;
    for the sake of your promise
    give me life. . . .
Your compassion is great, O LORD;
    in accord with your edicts give me life. . . .
Let my cry come before you, O LORD;
    in keeping with your word
    give me discernment.
Let my prayer come before you;
    rescue me according to your promise. . . .
Keep your hand ready to help me,
    for I have chosen your precepts. . . .
I have wandered like a lost sheep;
    seek out your servant,
    for I do not forget your commands.

My soul longs for your salvation;
I put my hope in your word.

From Psalm 120

The LORD answered me
when I called in my distress.

> The LORD answered me
> when I called in my distress:
> LORD, deliver me from lying lips,
> from treacherous tongues.

The LORD answered me
when I called in my distress.

FROM PSALM 121

God will not allow your foot to slip;
your guardian does not sleep.

> I raise my eyes toward the mountains.
>> From where will my help come?
>
> My help comes from the LORD,
>> the maker of heaven and earth.
>
> God will not allow your foot to slip;
>> your guardian does not sleep. . . .
>
> The LORD is your guardian;
>> the LORD is your shade
>>
>> at your right hand.
>
> By day the sun cannot harm you,
>> nor the moon by night.
>
> The LORD will guard you from all evil,
>> will always guard your life.
>
> The LORD will guard your coming and going
>> both now and forever.

God will not allow your foot to slip;
your guardian does not sleep.

FROM PSALM 123

Show us favor, LORD, show us favor.

> To you I raise my eyes,
>> to you enthroned in heaven.
> Yes, like the eyes of a servant
>> on the hand of his master,
> Like the eyes of a maid
>> on the hand of her mistress,
> So our eyes are on the LORD, our God,
>> till we are shown favor.
> Show us favor, LORD, show us favor,
>> for we have our fill of contempt.
> We have our fill of insult from the insolent,
>> of disdain from the arrogant.

Show us favor, LORD, show us favor.

FROM PSALM 124

Our help is the name of the LORD,
the maker of heaven and earth.

> . . . .Had not the LORD been with us,
>   when people rose against us,
> They would have swallowed us alive,
>   for their fury blazed against us.
> The waters would have engulfed us,
>   the torrent overwhelmed us;
>   seething waters would have drowned us.
> Blessed be the LORD who did not leave us
>   to be torn by their fangs.
> We escaped with our lives
>   like a bird from the fowler's snare;
>   the snare was broken and we escaped.
> Our help is the name of the LORD,
>   the maker of heaven and earth.

Our help is the name of the LORD,
the maker of heaven and earth.

FROM PSALM 125

Like Mount Zion are they
who trust in the LORD.

> Like Mount Zion are they
> who trust in the LORD,
> unshakable, forever enduring.
> As mountains surround Jerusalem,
> the LORD surrounds his people
> both now and forever. . . .
> Do good, LORD, to the good,
> to those who are upright of heart. . . .

Like Mount Zion are they
who trust in the LORD.

FROM PSALM 126

Restore again our fortunes, LORD.

> When the LORD restored the fortunes of Zion,
>> then we thought we were dreaming.
>
> Our mouths were filled with laughter;
>> our tongues sang for joy.
>
> Then it was said among the nations,
>> "The LORD has done great things for them."
>
> The LORD has done great things for us;
>> Oh, how happy we were!
>
> Restore again our fortunes, LORD,
>> like the dry stream beds of the Negeb.
>
> Those who sow in tears
>> will reap with cries of joy.
>
> Those who go forth weeping,
>> carrying sacks of seed,
>
> Will return with cries of joy,
>> carrying their bundled sheaves.

Restore again our fortunes, LORD.

FROM PSALM 127

Unless the LORD build the house,
they labor in vain who build.

> Unless the LORD build the house,
>   they labor in vain who build.
> Unless the LORD guard the city,
>   in vain does the guard keep watch.
> It is vain for you to rise early
>   and put off your rest at night,
> To eat bread earned by hard toil—
>   all this God gives to his beloved
>   in sleep. . . .

Unless the LORD build the house,
they labor in vain who build.

FROM PSALM 128

May the LORD bless you from Zion,
all the days of your life.

> Happy are all who fear the LORD,
>   who walk in the ways of God.
> What your hands provide you will enjoy;
>   you will be happy and prosper.
> Like a fruitful vine
>   your wife within your home,
> Like olive plants
>   Your children around your table.
> Just so will they be blessed
>   who fear the LORD.
> May the LORD bless you from Zion,
>   all the days of your life
> That you may share Jerusalem's joy
>   and live to see your
>   children's children. . . .

May the LORD bless you from Zion,
all the days of your life.

FROM PSALM 129

The just LORD cut me free.

> Much have they oppressed me from my youth,
>   now let Israel say.
> Much have they oppressed me from my youth,
>   yet they have not prevailed.
> Upon my back the plowers plowed,
>   as they traced their long furrows.
> But the just LORD cut me free
>   from the ropes of the yoke of the wicked.
> May they be scattered in disgrace,
>   all who hate Zion.
> May they be like grass on the rooftops
>   withered in early growth,
> Never to fill the reaper's hands,
>   nor the arms of the binders of sheaves,
> With none passing by to call out:
>   "The blessing of the LORD be upon you!
>   We bless you in the name of the LORD!"

The just LORD cut me free.

FROM PSALM 130

LORD, hear my cry!

> Out of the depths I call to you, LORD;
> LORD, hear my cry!
> May your ears be attentive
> to my cry for mercy. . . .
> I wait with longing for the LORD,
> my soul waits for his word.
> My soul looks for the LORD
> more than sentinels for daybreak,
> More than sentinels for daybreak,
> let Israel look for the LORD,
> For with the LORD is kindness,
> with him is full redemption. . . .

LORD, hear my cry!

FROM PSALM 131

LORD, my heart is not proud.

> LORD, my heart is not proud,
>   nor are my eyes haughty.
> I do not busy myself with great matters,
>   with things too sublime for me.
> Rather, I have stilled my soul,
>   hushed it like a weaned child.
> Like a weaned child on its mother's lap,
>   so is my soul within me.
> Israel, hope in the LORD,
>   now and forever.

LORD, my heart is not proud.

FROM PSALM 135

For the LORD defends his people,
shows mercy to his servants.

> Praise the name of the LORD!
>   Praise, you servants of the LORD,
> Who stand in the house of the LORD,
>   in the courts of the house of our God!
> Praise the LORD; the LORD is good!
>   Sing to God's name; it is gracious!
> I know that the LORD is great,
>   our LORD is greater than all gods.
> Whatever the LORD wishes
>   he does on heaven and on earth,
>   in the seas and in all the deeps.
> He raises storm clouds from
>   the end of the earth,
>   makes lightning and rain,
>   brings forth wind from the storehouse. . . .
> O LORD, your name is forever,
>   your renown, from age to age!
> For the LORD defends his people,
>   shows mercy to his servants. . . .

For the LORD defends his people,
shows mercy to his servants.

FROM PSALM 136

The LORD remembered us in our misery.

> Praise the LORD, who is so good;
>> God's love endures forever;
> Praise the God of gods;
>> God's love endures forever;
> Praise the LORD of LORDS;
>> God's love endures forever;
> Who alone has done great wonders,
>> God's love endures forever;
> Who skillfully made the heavens,
>> God's love endures forever;
> Who spread the earth upon the waters,
>> God's love endures forever;
> Who made the great lights,
>> God's love endures forever;
> The sun to rule the day,
>> God's love endures forever;
> The moon and stars to rule the night,
>> God's love endures forever;
> Who struck down the firstborn of Egypt;
>> God's love endures forever;
> And led Israel from their midst,
>> God's love endures forever;
> With mighty hand and outstretched arm,
>> God's love endures forever;

Who struck down the firstborn of Egypt,
  God's love endures forever;
Who split in two the Red Sea,
  God's love endures forever;
And led Israel through,
  God's love endures forever;
But swept Pharaoh and his army
  into the Red Sea,
  God's love endures forever;
Who led the people through the desert,
  God's love endures forever. . . .
The LORD remembered us in our misery,
  God's love endures forever;
Freed us from our foes,
  God's love endures forever;
And gives food to all flesh,
  God's love endures forever.
Praise the God of heaven,
  God's love endures forever.

The LORD remembered us in our misery.

From Psalm 138

When I cried out, you answered;
you strengthened my spirit.

> I thank you, LORD, with all my heart;
> before the gods to you I sing. . . .
> I praise your name for your fidelity
> and love.
> For you have exalted over all
> your name and your promise.
> When I cried out, you answered;
> you strengthened my spirit.
> All the kings of earth will praise you, LORD,
> when they hear the words of your mouth.
> They will sing of the ways of the LORD:
> "How great is the glory of the LORD!"
> The LORD is on high, but cares for the lowly
> and knows the proud from afar.
> Though I walk in the midst of dangers,
> you guard my life when my enemies rage.
> You stretch out your hand;
> your right hand saves me.
> The LORD is with me to the end.
> LORD, your love endures forever.
> Never forsake the work of your hands!

When I cried out, you answered;
you strengthened my spirit.

FROM PSALM 139

Probe me, God, know my heart;
try me, know my concerns.

> LORD, you have probed me, you know me;
>   you know when I sit and stand;
>   you understand my thoughts from afar.
> My travels and my rest you mark;
>   with all my words you are familiar.
> Even before a word is on my tongue,
>   LORD, you know it all.
> Behind and before you encircle me
>   and rest your hand upon me.
> Such knowledge is beyond me,
>   far too lofty for me to reach.
> Where can I hide from your spirit?
>   From your presence, where can I flee?
> If I ascend to the heavens, you are there;
>   if I lie down in Sheol, you are there, too.
> If I fly with the wings of dawn
>   and alight beyond the sea,
> Even there your hand will guide me,
>   your right hand hold me fast.
> If I say, "Surely darkness shall hide me,
>   and night shall be my light"—
> Darkness is not dark for you,
>   and night shines as the day.

Darkness and light are but one.
You formed my inmost being;
   you knit me in my mother's womb.
I praise you, so wonderfully you made me;
   wonderful are your works!
My very self you knew;
   my bones were not hidden from you,
When I was being made in secret,
   fashioned as in the depths of the earth.
Your eyes foresaw my actions;
   in your book all are written down;
   my days were shaped, before one came to be.
How precious to me are your designs, O God;
   how vast the sum of them!
Were I to count, they would outnumber
   the sands; to finish,
   I would need eternity. . . .
Probe me, God, know my heart;
   try me, know my concerns.
See if my way is crooked,
   then lead me in the ancient paths.

Probe me, God, know my heart;
try me, know my concerns.

FROM PSALM 140

Listen, LORD, to the words of my prayer.

> Deliver me, LORD, from the wicked;
>   preserve me from the violent,
> From those who plan evil in their hearts,
>   who stir up conflicts every day,
> Who sharpen their tongues like serpents. . . .
>   Keep me, LORD, from the clutches of the
> wicked; preserve me from the violent. . . .
> The arrogant have set a trap for me;
>   villains have spread a net,
>   laid snares for me by the wayside.
> I say to the LORD: You are my God;
>   listen, LORD, to the words of my prayer.
> My revered LORD, my strong helper,
>   my helmet on the day of battle.
> LORD, do not grant the desires of the wicked;
>   do not let their plots succeed. . . .
> Slanderers will not survive on earth;
>   evil will quickly entrap the violent.
> For I know the LORD will secure justice for
>   the needy, their rights for the poor.
> Then the just will give thanks to your name;
>   the upright will dwell in your presence.

Listen, LORD, to the words of my prayer.

FROM PSALM 141

My eyes are upon you, O God, my LORD.

> LORD, I call to you;
>   come quickly to help me;
>   listen to my plea when I call.
> Let my prayer be incense before you;
>   my uplifted hands an evening sacrifice. . . .
> My eyes are upon you, O God, my LORD;
>   in you I take refuge; do not strip me
>   of life.
> Guard me from the trap they have set for me,
>   from the snares of evildoers.
> Into their own nets let all the wicked fall,
>   while I make good my own escape.

My eyes are upon you, O God, my LORD.

FROM PSALM 142

Listen to my cry for help,
for I am brought very low.

> With full voice I cry to the LORD;
> with full voice I beseech the LORD.
> Before God I pour out my complaint,
> lay bare my distress.
> My spirit is faint within me. . . .
> I look to my right hand,
> but no friend is there.
> There is no escape for me;
> no one cares for me.
> I cry out to you, LORD,
> I say, You are my refuge,
> my portion in the land of the living.
> Listen to my cry for help,
> for I am brought very low.
> Rescue me from my pursuers,
> for they are too strong for me.
> Lead me out of my prison,
> that I may give thanks to your name.
> Then the just shall gather around me
> because you have been good to me.

Listen to my cry for help,
for I am brought very low.

From Psalm 143

Show me the path I should walk,
for to you I entrust my life.

> Lord, hear my prayer;
>> in your faithfulness listen to my pleading;
>> answer me in your justice.
>
> Do not enter into judgment with your servant;
>> before you no living being can be just.
>
> The enemy has pursued me;
>> they have crushed my life to the ground.
>
> They have left me in darkness
>> like those long dead.
>
> My spirit is faint within me;
>> my heart is dismayed.
>
> I remember the days of old;
>> I ponder all your deeds;
>> the works of your hands I recall.
>
> I stretch out my hands to you;
>> I thirst for you like a parched land.
>
> Hasten to answer me, Lord;
>> for my spirit fails me.
>
> Do not hide your face from me,
>> lest I become like those
>> descending to the pit.
>
> At dawn let me hear of your kindness,
>> for in you I trust.

Show me the path I should walk,
  for to you I entrust my life.
Rescue me, LORD, from my foes,
  for in you I hope.
Teach me to do your will,
  for you are my God.
May your kind spirit guide me
  on ground that is level.
For your name's sake, LORD, give me life;
  in your justice lead me out of distress. . . .

Show me the path I should walk,
for to you I entrust my life.

From Psalm 144

My safeguard and my fortress,
my stronghold, my deliverer.

> Blessed be the LORD, my rock,
>> who trains my hands for battle,
>> my fingers for war;
>
> My safeguard and my fortress,
>> my stronghold, my deliverer,
>
> My shield, in whom I trust,
>> who subdues peoples under me.
>
> LORD, what are mortals that you notice them;
>> human beings that you take thought of them?
>
> They are but a breath;
>> their days are like a passing shadow.
>
> LORD, incline your heavens and come;
>> touch the mountains and make them smoke.
>
> Flash forth lightning and scatter my foes;
>> shoot your arrows and rout them.
>
> Reach out your hand from on high;
>> deliver me from the many waters;
>> rescue me from the hands
>> of foreign foes. . . .
>
> O God. . . .
>
> You give victory to kings;
>> you delivered David, your servant.
>
> From the menacing sword deliver me;

rescue me from the hands
of foreign foes. . . .
May our sons be like plants
well nurtured from their youth,
Our daughters, like carved columns,
shapely as those of the temple.
May our barns be full
with every kind of store.
May our sheep increase by thousands,
by tens of thousands in our fields;
may our oxen be well fattened.
May there be no breach in the walls,
no exile, no outcry in the streets.
Happy the people so blessed;
happy the people whose God is the LORD.

My safeguard and my fortress,
my stronghold, my deliverer.

From Psalm 145

The LORD supports all who are falling
and raises up all who are bowed down.

> I will extol you, my God and king;
>> I will bless your name forever.
> Every day I will bless you;
>> I will praise your name forever.
> Great is the LORD and worthy of high praise;
>> God's grandeur is beyond understanding.
> One generation praises your deeds to the next
>> and proclaims your mighty works.
> They speak of the splendor
>> of your majestic glory,
>> tell of your wonderful deeds.
> They speak of your fearsome power
>> and attest to your great deeds.
> They publish the renown of your
>> abounding goodness
>> and joyfully sing of your justice.
> The LORD is gracious and merciful,
>> slow to anger and abounding in love.
> The LORD is good to all,
>> compassionate to every creature.
> All your works give you thanks, O LORD,
>> and your faithful bless you.
> They speak of the glory of your reign

and tell of your great works,
Making known to all your power,
  the glorious splendor of your rule.
Your reign is a reign for all ages,
  your dominion for all generations.
The LORD is trustworthy in every word,
  and faithful in every work.
The LORD supports all who are falling
  and raises up all who are bowed down.
The eyes of all look hopefully to you;
  you give them their food in due season.
You open wide your hand and satisfy
  the desire of every living thing.
You, LORD, are just in all your ways,
  faithful in all your works.
You, LORD, are near to all who call upon you,
  to all who call upon you in truth.
You satisfy the desire of those who fear you;
  you hear their cry and save them. . . .
My mouth will speak your praises, LORD;
  all flesh will bless your name forever.

The LORD supports all who are falling
and raises up all who are bowed down.

From Psalm 146

The LORD raises up those who are bowed down.

> Praise the LORD, my soul;
>> I shall praise the LORD all my life,
>> sing praise to my God while I live.
>
> Put no trust in princes,
>> in mere mortals powerless to save. . . .
>
> Happy those whose help is Jacob's God,
>> whose hope is in the LORD, their God,
>
> The maker of heaven and earth,
>> the seas and all that is in them,
>
> Who keeps faith forever,
>> secures justice for the oppressed,
>> gives food to the hungry.
>
> The LORD sets prisoners free;
>> the LORD gives sight to the blind.
>
> The LORD raises up those who are bowed down;
>> the LORD loves the righteous.
>
> The LORD protects the stranger,
>> sustains the orphan and the widow,
>> but thwarts the way of the wicked.
>
> The LORD shall reign forever. . . .

The LORD raises up those who are bowed down.

FROM PSALM 147

The LORD . . . heals the brokenhearted,
binds up their wounds.

> How good to celebrate our God in song;
>   how sweet to give fitting praise.
> The LORD rebuilds Jerusalem,
>   gathers the dispersed of Israel,
> Heals the brokenhearted,
>   binds up their wounds,
> Numbers all the stars,
>   calls each of them by name.
> Great is our LORD, vast in power,
>   with wisdom beyond measure.
> The LORD sustains the poor,
>   but casts the wicked to the ground.
> Sing to the LORD with thanksgiving;
>   with the lyre celebrate our God,
> Who covers the heavens with clouds,
>   provides rain for the earth,
>   makes grass sprout on the mountains,
>   who gives animals their food
>   and ravens what they cry for.
> God takes no delight in the strength
>   of horses,
>   no pleasure in the runner's stride.
> Rather, the LORD takes pleasure in the devout,

those who await his faithful care.
Glorify the LORD, Jerusalem;
  Zion, offer praise to your God,
  who has strengthened the bars
  of your gates,
  blessed your children within you,
Brought peace to your borders,
  and filled you with finest wheat.
The LORD sends a command to the earth;
  his word runs swiftly!
Thus snow is spread like wool,
  frost is gathered like ash,
Hail is dispersed like crumbs;
  before such cold the waters freeze.
Again he sends his word and they melt;
  the wind is unleashed and the waters flow.
The LORD also proclaims his word to Jacob,
  decrees and laws to Israel. . . .

The LORD . . . heals the brokenhearted,
binds up their wounds.

FROM PSALM 148

Praise the LORD.

> Praise the LORD from the heavens;
> give praise in the heights.
> Praise him, all you angels;
> give praise, all you hosts.
> Praise him, sun and moon;
> give praise, all shining stars.
> Praise him, highest heavens,
> you waters above the heavens.
> Let them all praise the LORD's name;
> for the LORD commanded
> and they were created,
> Assigned them duties forever,
> gave them tasks that will never change.
> Praise the LORD from the earth,
> you sea monsters and all deep waters;
> You lightning and hail, snow and clouds,
> storm winds that fulfill his command;
> You mountains and all hills,
> fruit trees and all cedars;
> You animals wild and tame,
> you creatures that crawl and fly;
> You kings of the earth and all peoples,
> princes and all who govern on earth;
> Young men and women, too,

old and young alike.
Let them all praise the LORD's name,
   for his name alone is exalted,
   majestic above earth and heaven.
The LORD has lifted high
   the horn [horn = strength] of his people;
   to the glory of all the faithful,
   of Israel, the people near to their God. . . .
Praise the LORD.

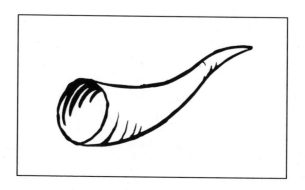

FROM PSALM 150

Let everything that has breath
give praise to the LORD!

> Praise God in his holy sanctuary;
>> give praise in the mighty dome of heaven.
>
> Give praise for his mighty deeds,
>> praise him for his great majesty.
>
> Give praise with blasts upon the horn,
>> praise him with harp and lyre.
>
> Give praise with tambourines and dance,
>> praise him with flutes and strings.
>
> Give praise with crashing cymbals,
>> praise him with sounding cymbals.
>
> Let everything that has breath
>> give praise to the LORD! Hallelujah!

Let everything that has breath
give praise to the LORD!